THE
SECRET SIDE
OF HISTORY

THE
SECRET SIDE
OF HISTORY

MYSTERY BABYLON AND
THE NEW WORLD ORDER

by
Dee Zahner

**LTAA COMMUNICATIONS
PUBLISHERS
HESPERIA, CALIFORNIA**

First Printing, August 1994
Second Printing, October 1996

Published by
LTAA Communications
P.O. Box 403092
Hesperia, California 92345
(619) 956-7640

Printed in the United States of America
Library of Congress Catalog Card Number: 95-90310
ISBN: 1-887017-01-1

**To my family
who helped make
this book possible**

Contents

Introduction

Beginning in the early 1960s, an increasing number of books and articles exposing the existence of a powerful world wide movement dedicated to creating a New World Order began to appear. Although the news media ignored these books and articles, as time passed, the media's own headlines bore out the worth of their allegations.

As the evidence accumulated, an amazing parallel to a world structure pictured in the seventeenth and eighteenth chapter of the Book of Revelation became apparent. This book is the result of viewing that unfolding parallel for nearly thirty years.

Since our subject deals in part with Bible prophecy, we wish to state at the very beginning that no Scriptural prophecy directs believers to acquiesce to evil. The admonition given in Romans 12:21 to, "Be not overcome of evil, but overcome evil with good" applies to all situations whenever and wherever evil appears.

Since the beginning of recorded history mankind has been involved in a continuous struggle between good and evil, between the spiritual forces of light and the spiritual forces of darkness. No place in Scripture is there an admonition for believers to be passive bystanders.

Throughout history those working for good have worked openly and often alone. Those working for evil have worked in secret and have usually been organized. Because of this, the secret side of history has often been the instigator of major world events.

Since as recorded in Luke 12:2, "For there is nothing covered, that shall not be revealed;..." those secrets eventually come to light. Unfortunately, this often occurs after the damage has been done. Although ignored by most historians, the secret side of history is usually the most important part of history. By the secret side of history we mean the behind-the-scenes forces, individuals, and decisions withheld from the general public.

This book seeks to stimulate readers to search out the organized forces behind contemporary events, and to use truth as a weapon against the perpetrators of evil deeds.

While doing so, it will be necessary not only to examine some of the men and organizations involved in today's secret side of history, it will be necessary also to examine some of the important individuals and organizations that are working to delay and eventually block the movement to lead the entire human race into a Satanic New World Order.

It may surprise our most perceptive readers to learn that the Apostle John, writing more than 1900 years ago, described the existence of a political and spiritual giant that parallels today's emerging New World Order. Not only did the Apostle describe its attributes and center of power ("that great city, which reigneth over the kings of the earth" Rev. 17:18) he also foretold its sudden loss of wealth and total destruction, all coming at a time when its leaders were at the height of their smug confidence. The Apostle labeled this evil center of world control "Mystery, Babylon The Great."

In order to show the similarity between Mystery Babylon's days and what has transpired during the twentieth century, we will detail the events of each period, events often on the secret side of history.

Lest our readers take refuge in Scripture's predicted fall of any Mystery Babylon, we hasten to quote an imperative command given to believers concerning this or any evil design for world power. In Revelation 18:4, the Apostle John relays this message:

> Come out of her, my people, that ye be not partakers of her sins, and that ye receive not of her plagues.

THE
SECRET SIDE
OF HISTORY

Chapter 1

Ancient Babylon

Is not this great Babylon, that I have built for the house of the kingdom by the might of my power, and for the honour of my majesty?

Daniel 4:30

This boast of Nebuchadnezzar in Daniel 4:30 was not an idle one; for Babylon was not only one of the most beautiful cities in the world, it was also the most powerful. Nebuchadnezzar (606-561 B.C.) had led it to the zenith of its power.

Located in an area many Bible scholars consider to be the cradle of the human race (the Euphrates-Tigris Valley, now part of Iraq), Babylon's history starts even before 2400 B.C. and goes back to the Tower of Babel. It was important enough to be mentioned in the Old Testament more than 250 times.

Before the discovery of the Behistun Rock in 1835 by Britain's Sir Henry Rawlinson, very little was known about Ancient Babylon outside of Old Testament history. On the face of this huge rock, 400 feet above a road, was found an inscription engraved in 516 B.C. by order of Darius, King of Persia, (521-485 B.C.). This was the same Darius who helped to rebuild the Temple at Jerusalem as recorded in the Book of Ezra.

The inscription contained a long account of the conquests of Darius written in the Persian, Elamite, and Babylonian languages. It provided the key to unlocking the vast treasure of ancient Babylonian literature.

Since then, scores of expeditions digging in the ruins of the Euphrates-Tigris Valley have unearthed hundreds of thousands of inscribed tablets and monuments. The dates of some of these show that the art of writing was known a thousand years before the time of Moses.

The most important discoveries have been found in the area where the Bible story began. This region was dotted with mounds containing the ruins of ancient cities. These mounds often reached a height of 100 feet and covered the remains of 20 cities, each built on top of the ruins of the previous one. Digging in these ruins, archaeologists have uncovered written history consistently confirming the accuracy of the Old Testament.

One of Babylon's early kings was Hammurabi who authored the famous code bearing his name 2000 B.C. He ruled over an advanced civilization that had written laws dealing with taxes, wages, public works, even international commerce. Discovered in 1902, Hammurabi's Code, written in stone, is now in the Louvre Museum in Paris. Hammurabi was a contemporary of Abraham, father of the Hebrew nation.

Abraham was also the father of the present Arab world through his son Ishmael. Abraham's life began in Ur, one of the prominent cities in Ancient Babylon.

Ancient historians have told us that, at the height of its glory, Babylon was protected by 60 miles of walls, 15 miles on each side. The walls were 300 feet high, 80 feet thick at their base and sunk to a depth of 35 feet below ground. On the walls were 250 towers with housing for military personnel. Through 100 brass gates passed traffic in and out of the city. Deep and wide canals surrounded the outside of the walls.

Inside the outer wall there was another barrier made of two parallel walls each 20 feet thick. The inner wall was also protected by a canal. A quarter of a mile farther in from the inner wall lay the city. In times of ancient warfare it was simply impregnable. Excavations of recent years seem to verify the fabulous accounts of historians. It was a beautiful city with the Euphrates River flowing through the center. Its hanging gardens were one of the Seven Wonders of the ancient world. Isaiah called it, "Babylon, the glory of kingdoms,..." Isaiah 13:19.

The Old Testament prophet Jeremiah lived during the time of Nebuchadnezzar. During this period the moral level of Judah had fallen so low that the prophet repeatedly cried out against the evil of his day, prophesying the coming captivity of the nation of Judah by the Babylonians.

Eventually the predictions of Jeremiah did come to pass as recorded in II Kings chapter 24:

11 And Nebuchadnezzar King of Babylon came against the city, and his servants did besiege it.

> 14 And he carried away all Jerusalem, and all the princes, and all the mighty men of valor, even ten thousand captives, and all the craftsmen and smiths; none remained, save the poorest sort of the people of the land.

This was history's first recorded deportation. Later, during the reign of King Zedekiah, the Babylonians returned, destroyed the city of Jerusalem, and took the remaining inhabitants captive to Babylon.

Daniel was in the first group of captives taken from Jerusalem to Babylon (606 B.C.). Here he spent the rest of his life (70 years). Although unswerving in his own religious convictions, Daniel held high positions in the government under several Babylonian kings. It was in this city that Daniel was thrown into the lion's den, and Shadrack, Meshack, and Abed-nego were cast into the fiery furnace.

Twelve manuscripts of Isaiah and fragments of the Book of Daniel were found among the Dead Sea Scrolls. The first discovery of these scrolls in 1947 led to the exploration of eleven caves near the Dead Sea. Altogether, these efforts yielded hundreds of manuscripts dating from the last century B.C. and first century A.D. This find has been hailed as one of the most important discoveries of Old Testament manuscripts. Many works found during this period have been published and are available for study either in translation or in facsimile. These scrolls substantiate the historical events of the Old Testament as recorded by Isaiah and Daniel.

Babylon was a national center of idolatry. Its chief deity was Marduk (Bel), a name given to Nimrod. Nimrod may have been the builder of the Tower of Babel. The temple of Marduk contained golden images of Bel and Ishtar including a human figure of solid gold 18 feet high. Babylon had 53 temples, and 180 altars dedicated to Ishtar.

Ishtar was worshiped as a moon-goddess. She was a deification of the sex passion and worshipping her required licentiousness. Sacred prostitution within her sanctuaries was a universal custom among the women of Babylon. Every maid, wife or widow had to officiate in these rites at least once in her lifetime . The prophet Isaiah gives us a good look into the heart and soul of Babylon in Isaiah chapter 47:

> 8 Therefore hear now this, thou that art given to pleasures, that dwellest carelessly, that sayest in thine heart, I am, and none beside me....
>
> 9 But these two things shall come upon thee in a moment in one day, the loss of children, and widowhood: they shall come upon thee in their perfection for the multitude of thy sorceries, and for the great abundance of thine enchantments.
>
> 10 For thou hast trusted in thy wickedness: thou has said, None seeth me.

Although Ancient Babylon was outwardly powerful she was inwardly corrupt, a condition that led to her downfall. As foretold by Isaiah and Jeremiah, the fall came very suddenly during a time when her leaders felt totally secure.

Scripture records that during a feast for a thousand of his lords, King Belshazzar called for the vessels that Nebuchadnezzar had taken out of the temple in Jerusalem. At the very hour when the king and his guests drank out of the sacred vessels and praised their gods, the fingers of a man's hand appeared and wrote a message upon the plaster of the palace wall. It was a message announcing that God had decreed an end to the Babylonian kingdom. The entire story is related in Daniel chapter 5, drawing the curtain down in verses 30 and 31:

> In that night was Belshazzar king of the Chaldeans slain.
> And Darius the Median took the kingdom, being about three score and two years old.

What had taken place, as recorded by ancient historians, is related in *Halley's Bible Handbook*:

> The Fall of Babylon is thus related by Xenophon, Herodotus and Berosus: "Cyrus diverted the Euphrates into a new channel, and guided by two deserters, marched by the dry bed into the city, while the Babylonians were carousing at a feast of their gods."[1]

The city fell without a battle; and today Ancient Babylon, as prophesied by Isaiah a hundred years before it rose to the zenith of its power, is nothing more than a heap of ruins. Many bricks from these ruins were used in building Baghdad the capital of Iraq. It is of interest that Alexander the Great wished to restore Babylon, but his plans were cut short by his early death.

Referring to Babylon, Isaiah stated that, "It shall never be inhabited, neither shall it be dwelt in from generation to generation:..." Isaiah 13:20.

Although Saddam Hussein rebuilt a small section and has used this as a psychological rallying point for his followers, the ancient city has no foreseeable major significance in the commercial or political world. Its significance lies in its amazing parallel to the Mystery Babylon of Revelation, and to the movement in the world today called The New World Order.

Chapter 2

Mystery Babylon

> And upon her forehead was a name written, MYSTERY, BABYLON THE GREAT, THE MOTHER OF HARLOTS AND ABOMINATIONS OF THE EARTH.
>
> Revelation 17:5

> And the woman which thou sawest is that great city, which reigneth over the kings of the earth.
>
> Revelation 17:18

Although the Babylon of Revelation is literally identified as "Babylon The Great" with the word "Mystery," attached to it, for the purpose of illustration and comparison, we have chosen to identify it as "Mystery Babylon" as is done in the *New International Version* of the *Bible*. Clearly, both terms describe the Babylon of Revelation.

The writer of the Book of Revelation gave no geographical location or time period of the great city that was described as reigning over the kings of the earth. He did, however, give a detailed description of its character and its deeds.

The word "mystery" as applied to Babylon is a Greek word μυστήριον (Musterion) that carries the idea of silence or secrecy imposed by initiation into religious rites. The root word μύω (Muo) means to shut the mouth. A good interpretation would be Secret Babylon.

What is inferred here is that secret organizations would accumulate enough power to rule over the rulers of the world and at the same time keep their control hidden from public view. Ancient Babylon ruled openly, Mystery Babylon rules secretly. The name of Babylon was probably given to this center of world power because of its similarities to Ancient Babylon. Following is a list of those similarities.

1. Both ruled the world:

> And the woman which thou sawest is that great city, which reigneth over the kings of the earth.
> Revelation 17:18

2. Both were exceedingly rich:

> And saying, Alas, alas, that great city, that was clothed in fine linen, and purple, and scarlet, and decked with gold, and precious stones, and pearls!
> Revelation 18:16

3. Both receive a prophecy of judgement:

> For in one hour so great riches is come to nought.
> Revelation 18:17

4. Both were great centers of commerce.

And they cast dust on their heads, and cried, weeping and wailing, saying, Alas, alas, that great city, wherein were made rich all that had ships in the sea by reason of her costliness!

Revelation 18:19

5. Both were allied with spiritual evil.

And the light of a candle shall shine no more at all in thee; and the voice of the bridegroom and of the bride shall be heard no more at all in thee: for thy merchants were the great men of the earth; for by thy sorceries were all nations deceived.

Revelation 18:23

6. Both killed great numbers, especially believers.

And in her was found the blood of prophets, and of saints, and of all that were slain upon the earth.

Revelation 18:24

7. Both were a corrupting influence.

For true and righteous are his judgments: for he hath judged the great whore, which did corrupt the earth with her fornication, . . .

Revelation 19:2

In condemning Ancient Babylon, the Old Testament prophet Jeremiah used language very similar to that used in the condemnation of Mystery Babylon. Many of these verses are found in the 51st chapter of Jeremiah.

As in the case of Ancient Babylon, Mystery Babylon's fall comes suddenly and at a time when its leaders are confident of their security:

> How much she hath glorified herself, and lived deliciously, so much torment and sorrow give her: for she saith in her heart, I sit a queen, and am no widow, and shall see no sorrow.
>
> Revelation 18:7

> Therefore shall her plagues come in one day, death, and mourning, and famine; . . .
>
> Revelation 18:8

While Ancient Babylon and Mystery Babylon constitute an amazing parallel, there is another far more important parallel. This is the parallel of Mystery Babylon and a world structure that has been built in this century and has as its goal the total subjugation of the human race under a New World Order.

For purpose of comparison, we have chosen to label this present world structure as Modern Day Babylon. In order to illustrate its parallel to Mystery Babylon, we will examine some of the events occurring on the secret side of history from ancient times to the present.

Chapter 3

Ancient Oral Traditions

Hide me from the secret counsel of the wicked; from
the insurrection of the workers of iniquity: . . .

Psalm 64:2

Since early times, "Wise Men" have existed who
claimed knowledge of "Mysteries" that were to be kept
secret from all outside their circle. Some of these
mysteries purported to relate to such matters as the origin
of man, life of the soul after death, and the nature of
God. These mysteries were usually handed down by oral
tradition and kept from the ordinary people.

Many Jewish writers believe that Moses drew from
the Egyptian Mysteries a part of an oral tradition handed
down through the leaders of the Israelites (the Jews), and
later written in the Talmud and the Cabala. Others
believe that an oral tradition goes back to Adam. There
was a conflict here, and it could be found not only in
traditions, but in the resulting polarization of the Jews
with one side supporting orthodox Judaism and one side
working to undermine it.

That there existed a secret oral tradition claiming to
be the teaching of Moses, but contrary to the Law, could
explain why many Jewish people were so quick to
forsake the written Law of Moses and join in worshiping

the deities of the heathen nations around them.

Acceptance of the worship of heathen deities often led to grossly immoral practices, even to human sacrifice as in the worship of Molech. It is a sad commentary that even Solomon fell into idol worship in his old age (I Kings 11:1-8).

After the death of Solomon the kingdom was divided into the Northern Kingdom of ten tribes (Israel) and the Southern Kingdom of two tribes (Judah). Immediately, Israel rejected the Law of Moses and turned to worship of the Golden Calf, an Egyptian deity. The Northern Kingdom lasted about 200 years until it was destroyed by Assyria in 721 B.C. Every one of its 19 kings followed the worship of the Golden Calf.

Judah, the Southern Kingdom, lasted slightly more than 300 years, and as was noted previously, was destroyed by Babylon about 600 B.C. Most of its Kings also worshiped idols. Only a few revered the Law of Moses.

That there was indeed a secret movement behind the rejection of the Law of Moses is attested to in the writings of Old Testament prophets. Jeremiah denounced the existence of such a movement in his day. This is recorded in Jeremiah 11:9-10:

> And the Lord said unto me, A conspiracy is found among the men of Judah, and among the inhabitants of Jerusalem.

> They are turned back to the iniquities of their forefathers, which refused to hear my words; and they went after other gods to serve them: . . .

The Old Testament prophet Ezekiel also lamented such a movement in Israel:

> There is a conspiracy of her prophets in the midst thereof, like a roaring lion ravening the prey; they have devoured souls; they have taken the treasure and precious things; they have made her many widows in the midst thereof.
>
> Ezekiel 22:25

These conspiracies so corrupted Judah and Israel that the two nations were conquered, and their people taken away into slavery by Assyria and Babylon.

Intellectuals often scoff at the mention of conspiracy, but it is impossible to believe the Scriptures and not believe in conspiracies. Conspiracies are mentioned thirty times in the Old Testament, often in connection with the overthrow, or attempted overthrow, of existing governments.

The existence of secret oral traditions among the Jews could well explain some of the language of the New Testament. In John 7:49 for example, the Pharisees said, "But this people who knoweth not the law are cursed." Yet, the people did know the written law. At this time in the history of the Jews, the Law was revered by the common people and regularly read to them in the synagogues on the Sabbath. The Pharisees were likely referring to an oral tradition unknown to the common people.

In Matthew 23:15 Jesus condemned the Pharisees for the corrupting of their followers:

> Woe unto you scribes and Pharisees, hypocrites! for ye compass sea and land to make one proselyte, and when he is made, ye make him twofold more the child of hell than yourselves.

If the proselyte had been taught the written Law of Moses, such a condemnation would not have been likely. However, instruction in a secret oral tradition could account for evil practices that would merit condemnation. At another time, Jesus may have stopped just short of exposing what the Pharisees were secretly teaching. This is recorded in Luke 12:1-3:

> In the mean time, when there were gathered an innumerable multitude of people, insomuch that they trode one upon another, he began to say unto his disciples first of all, Beware ye of the leaven of the Pharisees, which is hypocrisy.
>
> For there is nothing covered, that shall not be revealed; neither hid, that shall not be known.
>
> Therefore whatsoever ye have spoken in darkness shall be heard in the light; and that which ye have spoken in the ears in closets shall be proclaimed upon the housetops.

In the minds of the Pharisees such a condemnation may have been a warning that public exposure could follow, thus galvanizing their determination to destroy Jesus.

However the case, there did exist at the time of Christ, an assemblage of doctrines and speculations that were carefully concealed from the multitude. For the most part these doctrines (contained in the Jewish Cabala) were directed against orthodox Judaism. The word "cabala" comes from a Hebrew word that signifies "a doctrine orally received." Although the date is uncertain, these doctrines were eventually written in what is now known as the *Zohar*.

After the establishment of Christianity, slanders on Christ and Christians occurred in some versions of the Cabala. On the other hand, the Koran, the holy book of the Muslims, denounces the infamous legends concerning Christ perpetuated by the Jews.

Chapter 4

Secret Societies

The wicked, through the pride of his countenance,
will not seek God: God in not in all his thoughts.
Psalms 10:4

He sitteth in the lurking places of the villages: in the
secret places doth he murder the innocent: . . .
Psalms 10:8

He lieth in wait secretly as a lion in his den: . . .
Psalm 10:9

To understand the establishment of a power as evil and extensive as Mystery Babylon, it is helpful to consider some secret societies and conspiracies that have determined the outcome of many historical events. Their existence is as old as mankind.

The British historian, Nesta H. Webster, relates their beginning in this manner:

The East is the cradle of secret societies. For whatever end they may have been employed, the inspiration and methods of these mysterious associations which have played so important a part behind the scenes of the world's history will be found to have emanated from the lands where the first recorded acts of the great human drama were played out — Egypt, Babylon, Syria, and Persia. On the one hand Eastern mysticism, on the other Oriental love of intrigue, framed the systems later to be transported to the West with results so tremendous and far-reaching.[1]

Much of the suffering of the human race has come about as a result of those secret societies and their successors. The "results so tremendous and far reaching" referred to by Webster have been a disaster for the well-being of the inhabitants of planet earth, and have repeatedly blocked spiritual and material progress.

The British historian, John Robison, (1798) had this to say about secret societies:

> But not only are secret societies dangerous, but all societies whose object is mysterious. The whole history of man is a proof of this position. In no age or country has there ever appeared a mysterious association which did not in time become a public nuisance.[2]

An examination of a few of the secret societies existing during the middle ages gives an insight into the general duplicity and propensity for evil common to secret societies.

One of the prominent secret societies of this period was an order know as The Assassins. In this order drugs were used to recruit young men to become professional assassins in order to forward the designs of their masters.

The young man whom the Assassins desired to recruit was introduced to the Grand Master of the Order and drugged. While unconscious, he was carried into a beautiful garden with luxurious resting places. Here amid sparkling streams, fruit trees, and flowers he was attended by beautiful women serving him wine in gold and silver vessels as soft music played in the background.

After enjoying all the delights of what he believed was paradise, he was again drugged and, while once more unconscious, carried back to the presence of the Grand Master. Upon awakening, he was assured that he had never left the side of the Grand Master but had merely experienced a foretaste of the paradise that awaited him if he obeyed the orders of his masters.

In this matter the Assassins established a system of organized murder on a basis of religious fervor, and unleashed a reign of terror throughout the East. Years later, in secret records released by two of their own leaders, a list was found of celebrated men of all nations who had been their victims.

Eventually, the leaders of the Assassins turned on each other and became the victims of the poisons and daggers they had prepared for others. Although the dynasty of the Assassins had ended by 1250, the sects from which they derived continued.

The Knights Templar is another example of the end results of secret societies. After the First Crusade had ended with the defeat of the Muslims and the capture of Jerusalem, a band of nine Frenchmen formed an order (in 1118) for the protection of pilgrims to the Holy Sepulchre. The King of Jerusalem presented them with a house near the Temple of Solomon resulting in the name Knights Templar. The Templars were bound by a vow of poverty and were to live solely on alms. But donations became so enormous that they eventually abandoned their vow of poverty and spread themselves over Europe. By the end of the twelfth century they had become a rich and powerful body.

By the end of the thirteenth century the rumors of their unscrupulous deeds and low moral life caused them to become suspect in the eyes of the clergy and the general public, word of their apostasy even reaching the Pope.

On October 13, 1307, the King of France had all of the Templars in France arrested. Many confessed that they had been ordered to spit on the crucifix and had been urged to commit obscenities and practice unnatural vice. Later, and without duress of any kind, these confessions were repeated before the Pope by seventy-two of the French Knights.

Similar to other secret societies, the Templars had a double doctrine. The one presented to the majority of members at the lower level, and to the public, was replete with noble endeavors. If a member was able to ascend to a higher level by proving to his unscrupulous superiors that he could be trusted to keep their secrets and carry out their orders, he was told more about the true purpose of the order. These evil designs were most often communicated orally. The outward profession contained nothing but perfect orthodoxy. The inside or secret profession was anti-Christian.

Some writers believed that the Templars believed in a god of good and a god of evil but chose to serve the god of evil (Lucifer) because they thought him to be more powerful and able to make them rich. Nesta H. Webster gives the following quotation:

> Their most fervent worship was addressed to this god of evil, who alone could enrich them. "They said with the Luciferians: The elder son of God, Satanael or Lucifer alone has a right to the homage of mortals; Jesus his younger brother does not deserve this honour."[3]

The Templars not only became international bankers in their day, they also supported uprisings against existing governments to a point of threatening world wide revolution. As we progress to our study of the Mystery Babylon of Revelation, we will see that history repeats itself.

It has been tragic for the human race that secret societies, with a small number of leaders always operating in secrecy, have been able to involve large numbers of well-meaning followers at the lower levels who, in working for the goals of the organization, were paving the way for their own destruction. This pattern is more evident in the twentieth century than at any other time in history.

Just as there existed secret and subversive sects working against Christianity and orthodox Judaism, there were also secret movements organized for the purpose of undermining all moral and religious beliefs in the minds of Muslims. These began in the middle of the seventh century resulting in an immense schism in Islam that led to open warfare.

An important faction to rise out of the many splits was the Ismailis who up to about A.D. 872 remained believers. At this time Abdullah ibn Maymun, an intriguer of extraordinary cunning, succeeded in capturing control of the movement which then became subversive, not only of Islamism, but of all religious beliefs. The Ismailis movement became a model for the organization of modern secret societies.

The first open acts of violence resulting from the doctrines of Abdullah were carried out by the Karmathites, a secret society named after its leader Karmath. Karmath, a born schemer who believed in nothing, became the leader of the Karmathites in Arabia where a number of Arabs were soon enlisted in the society.

Karmath persuaded his followers to give all of their money to him and establish a community of goods and wives. Becoming absolute master of their minds, he led them away from all religion and released them from all the duties of piety, devotion, and the fear of God. This was just the opposite of what he had prescribed for them before they were "enlightened."

He permitted them pillage (robbery by violent means), and every sort of immoral license, teaching that they could pillage the goods and shed the blood of their adversaries with impunity.

Peaceful fraternity was thus turned into a wild lust for conquest as the Karmathites became a band of robbers, pillaging and massacring throughout all the surrounding districts. Nesta Webster quotes von Kammer as saying:

> For a whole century the pernicious doctrines of Karmath raged with fire and sword in the very bosom of Islamism, until the wide spread conflagration was extinguished in blood.[4]

Chapter 5

The Illuminati

For we wrestle not against flesh and blood, but against principalities, against powers, against the rulers of the darkness of this world, against spiritual wickedness in high places.

Ephesians 6:12

The organization that has had the greatest impact upon events occurring since the later part of the 18th century is a secret society founded in Bavaria in 1776. Its founder, Adam Weishaupt, a professor of canon law at the University of Ingolstadt, labeled it the Illuminati Order.

The pretended purpose of the Order was to bring universal happiness to the human race by promoting world brotherhood and equality. The true purpose of the Order, hidden behind layers of secrecy, was to rule the world. To achieve this goal the Order set out to destroy all religion, overthrow all governments, and abolish all existing social order, such as the family and ownership of private property. This plan has been followed by the Communists since 1848.

Using the methods of earlier secret societies, Weishaupt, through his organizing ability, was able to make the Illuminati one of the most effective instruments of evil that has ever been uncovered. Using the philosophy that "the end justifies the means," his methods became a model for world revolution.

Eventually, the Order became suspect by the government of Bavaria, resulting in an investigation by a Bavarian Court of Inquiry in 1783. An event that led to exposure of the subversive nature of the Order was the untimely death of one of its members, an evangelist preacher named Lanze, who, while on a mission to Silesia, was struck down by lightning. Instructions found on his body resulted in a raid on the houses of two of the leading members of the Order. Here much incriminating evidence was uncovered, among which was a list of poisons.

Although Weishaupt was banished from Bavaria, and the Order was officially suppressed, the Order simply went underground and emerged as a network of Reading Societies throughout Germany. The goal of this network was to monopolize the writing, publication, reviewing, and distribution of all literature, as a means of controlling the minds of the readers.

From the very beginning, the Illuminati was a secret society within a secret society, beginning in the Masonic Lodge Theodore of Munich, Germany of which Weishaupt was a member. It was his plan to use the

Freemasons as a recruiting ground, and as a vehicle to propagate his philosophy.

Masonic Lodges in France and Germany during the 18th century became breeding grounds for revolution. Ideological evolution within the French lodges brought forth the Jacobin Clubs of revolutionary fame.

It is important to distinguish between Freemasonry in Europe, especially France, from Freemasonry in England and America where, historically, and today, its members are usually characterized by high standards of morality and spirituality.

To recruit members into the Order Weishaupt advised his followers to:

> Seek out young and already skillful people. . . . Our people must be engaging, enterprising, intriguing, and adroit. Above all the first.[1]

The Order did not overlook the usefulness of enlisting women in their cause, as evidenced by their written directives:

> There is no way of influencing men so powerfully as by means of the women. These should therefore be our chief study; we should insinuate ourselves into their good opinion, give them hints of emancipation from tyranny of public opinion, and of standing up for themselves; it will be an immense relief to their enslaved minds to be freed from any one bond of restraint, and it will fire them the more, and cause them to work for us with zeal, without knowing that they do so; . . . [2]

Membership in the Order was based upon a series of "degrees" or levels of enlightenment with only the bold and ruthless reaching the top and learning the true purpose of the Order. Upon joining, members were required to take an oath swearing blind obedience to their superiors, surrender of their own will, and perpetual silence. Through a system of required autobiographies and internal spying, the superiors carefully selected those suited for advancement to higher degrees.

Secret police were organized and used to assassinate those members who went astray. Their symbol was an eye above a pyramid, the same as appears on the back of the U.S. one dollar bills.

As was the case with secret societies, the real leaders hid their identity, thus Weishaupt wrote:

> My circumstances necessitate, . . . that I should remain hidden from most of the members as long as I live. I have two immediately below me into whom I breathe my whole spirit, and each of these two has again two others, and so on. In this way I can set a thousand men in motion and on fire in the simplest manner, and in this way one must impart orders and operate on politics.[3]

> The great strength of our Order lies in its concealment; let it never appear in any place in its own name, but always covered by another name, and another occupation.[4]

A prime target for the Illuminati was the control of the schools, libraries, printing-houses, bookshops, and any other avenue that served to mold public opinion. Their stated objectives were:

> We must acquire the direction of education — of church-management — of the professional chair, and of the pulpit. We must bring our opinions into fashion by every art . . . [5]

To insure secrecy in their private correspondence, leaders of the Order took ancient names. Weishaupt was Spartacus, Zwack (a judge) was Cato, and so on. Members were advised to practice writing with both hands to further obscure their identity. The secrets of the Order were so well guarded that no one outside of a small circle knew that Weishaupt was the head of the Order until its papers were seized in 1786.

Their attitude toward religion was to profess Christianity while working to destroy it. They taught that, rather than God creating the universe, the universe is creating God and that man is himself god and therefore unaccountable to a higher power. This is similar to the New Age doctrine of the 20th century.

They also taught that Jesus had a secret doctrine, a doctrine of reason that only the enlightened could understand. Rather than being a redeemer, Jesus was only a teacher whose purpose was to unite men in a great universal association thereby leading men to universal liberty and equality.

Weishaupt was such a master at perverting Christian doctrine that he gleefully boasted of the acceptance of his Priest degree:

> You can't imagine what respect and curiosity my priest-degree has raised; and, which is wonderful, a famous Protestant divine, who is now of the Order, is persuaded that the religion contained in it is the true sense of Christianity. O MAN, MAN! TO WHAT MAY'ST THOU NOT BE PERSUADED. Who would imagine that I was to be the founder of a new religion.[6]

And what of the moral character of these molders of the minds of men and would be rulers of the world? For an answer we turn to their own confessions. In a letter to Cato (Zwack) Spartacus (Weishaupt) writes:

> What shall I do? I am deprived of all help. Socrates, who would insist on being a man of consequence among us, and is really a man of talents, and of a right way of thinking, is eternally besotted. Augustus is in the worst estimation imaginable. Alcibiades sits the day long with the vintner's pretty wife, and there he sighs and pines. A few days ago, at Corinth, Tiberius attempted to ravish the wife of Democides, and her husband came in upon them. . . . When the worthy man Marcus Aurelius comes to Athens (Munich) what will he think? What a meeting with dissolute immoral wretches, whore-masters, liars, bankrupts, braggarts, and vain fools![7]

In a letter to Marius in September 1783, Weishaupt writes:

> I am now in the most embarrassing situation; it robs
> me of all rest, and makes me unfit for every thing. I am
> in danger of losing at once my honor and my reputation,
> by which I have long had such influence. What think you
> — my sister-in-law is with child. . . . We have tried every
> method in our power to destroy the child; . . . [8]

And what of the accomplishments of this collection of "immoral wretches, whore-masters, liars, bankrupts, braggarts, and vain fools?" In just a decade, membership included about 600 of the most influential men in Bavaria. Below are excerpts from a report written in Cato's handwriting:

> By the activity of our Brethren, the Jesuits have been
> kept out of all the professional chairs at Ingolstadt, and
> our friends prevail.
> The Widow Duchess has set up her academy entirely
> according to our plan, and we have all the Professors in
> the Order.
> Our Ghostly Brethren have been very fortunate this
> last year, for we have procured for them several good
> benefices, parishes, tutorships, &c.
> All the German Schools, and the Benevolent Society,
> are at last under our direction. [9]

> We have got several zealous members in the courts
> of justice, and we are able to afford them pay, and other
> good additions.

Lately, we have got possession of the Bartholomew Institution for young clergymen, having secured all its supporters. Through this we shall be able to supply Bavaria with fit priests.[10]

Those who were willing to become tools of the Order were rewarded for their mindless obedience to their unknown superiors by the following policy:

The power of the Order must surely be turned to the advantage of its Members. All must be assisted. They must be preferred to all persons otherwise of equal merit. Money, services, honor, goods, and blood, must be expended for the fully proved Brethren, and the unfortunate must be relieved by the funds of the Society.[11]

Thus the conspirators lived well while the fruits of their labor culminated in heartache, poverty, and every form of human suffering for the unfortunate souls living through the wars, revolutions, unrest, and turmoil created by these self-appointed perpetrators of "happiness for the human race."

Chapter 6

The French Revolution

Ye are of your father the devil, and the lusts of your father ye will do. He was a murderer from the beginning, and abode not in the truth, because there is no truth in him. When he speaketh a lie, he speaketh of his own: for he is a liar, and the father of it.

John 8:44

Here, in a stinging indictment delivered to the Jews who were seeking to kill Him, Jesus identified the primary source of falsehood and murder as Satanic. As we progress through events of the French Revolution it will become evident that the primary motivation, beyond lust for wealth and power, was a Satanically-inspired desire of evil for the sake of evil.

After firmly establishing themselves in Bavaria (a part of what is now Germany), the leaders of the Illuminati began to work toward their international goal of overthrowing all existing governments and, eventually, ruling the world.

At that time (1789) France was the richest and most populous nation on the continent of Europe; and it was here that the "great experiment in Democracy" began. The battle cry was "liberty, equality, and fraternity." The vehicle was Socialism.

That the French Revolution was a model for Socialist revolution was expressed by the anarchist Prince Kropotkin in 1908:

> What we learn to-day from the study of the Great Revolution, . . . is that it was the source and origin of all the present communist, anarchist, and socialist conceptions. . . . up till now, modern socialism has added absolutely nothing to the ideas that were circulating among the French people between 1789 and 1794, and which it was tried to put into practice in the year II. of the Republic. Modern socialism has only systematized those ideas and found arguments in their favor, . . . [1]

Indeed, the French Revolution was a source for communist, anarchist, and socialist conceptions; conceptions that, when carried to conclusion, resulted in the necessity of installing drainage systems to carry away the torrents of blood that flowed from French guillotines. These same "conceptions" applied during the twentieth century have resulted in the murder of well over one hundred million human beings. There is much to learn from the Great Revolution. Commenting on the Revolution, the British historian Nesta Webster wrote:

> If, then, we would discover the truth about these great revolutionary outbreaks, we must dig down far below the surface, we must trace the connection between the mine and the explosion, between the actions of the people and the causes that provoked them. [2]

Although ignored by most historians, especially those who wished to glorify the leaders of the Revolution, the truth was recorded by all factions, and preserved in primary source documents. These documents have been available to all who wished to present the truth about this dark period in world history.

Lord Acton said, "The appalling thing in the French Revolution is not the tumult but the design."[3] The design that is apparent throughout the Revolution is Adam Weishaupt's plan to destroy all religion, overthrow all governments, and rule the world.

Tragically, the Revolution began at a time when great progress was being made toward the reforms sought by the people. The force behind the movement for reform was not the revolutionaries, but King Louis XVI.

To ascertain the wishes of the people, a proclamation had been sent out by the King to the whole nation saying:

> His Majesty has desired that in the extremities of his kingdom and in the obscurest dwellings every man shall rest assured that his wishes and requests shall be heard.[4]

The lists of grievances that arrived from all parts of the country were compiled in what was known as the "cahiers." The contents of the cahiers were summed up by Hua that:

> The voice of the nation cried out for reform, for changes in the government, but all proclaimed respect

for religion, loyalty to the King, and desire for law and order.[5]

Unfortunately, peaceful reform was not to be the fate of France. Plans for violent revolution were already far advanced by what was to become known as the Orleaniste Conspiracy.

The principal character in the Orleaniste Conspiracy was the Duke of Orleans, a nobleman of great wealth who had been recruited into the Illuminati by Mirabeau. Lured into supporting the Revolution by the hope of attaining the throne in place of his cousin, Louis XVI, and driven by his hatred of the Queen, Marie Antoinette, the Duke of Orleans became a most willing tool of the conspiracy.

Though hailed as "the idol of Paris," the Duke of Orleans was actually loathed and despised by the people. This was partly due to his low moral character and partly to his disdain for the people. It was no small task for the party that supported him to convince the people that the man who treated them with insolence had become their champion of liberty.

The election of the Duke of Orleans to Grand Master of the Masonic Order in France was the crowning success of the Illuminati's plan (plotted by Mirabeau) to infiltrate Freemasonry and to use it as a base of operations in promoting violent revolution. Out of these Masonic lodges in France came the organization known as the Jacobin Clubs. These clubs provided the leadership for the events of the French Revolution.

In the beginning and throughout the Revolution, a campaign of vilification was carried out against the King and Queen, the priests and nobles. These vilifications took the part of both written slanders and oral harangues calculated to stir up class hatred among the people. This form of propaganda was simply the implementation of the big lie technique.

In addition to propaganda, it was necessary to create a crisis to contribute to the restlessness of the people. This was accomplished by the agents of the Duke of Orleans buying up the grain supplies and withholding them from the people. By this means the threat of famine faced the people and the cry of "bread" was added to the cry of liberty and equality. To add to the agitation of the people, the scarcity of grain was blamed on the King and Nobles as monopolizers. Throughout the Revolution this tactic — of always blaming your enemy for what you are doing — was used.

But in order to start the blood of the revolution flowing it was necessary to go a step farther, the hiring of criminals and ruffians. These brigands from the South of France and Italy, known as the Marseillais, began flocking into Paris in the spring of 1789. Men of ferrous appearance, they carried thick knotted sticks and made up the hard core of the major uprisings that were to follow.

To swell a mob of insurrection, these brigands would go into the factories and workshops and compel the workers to follow them. On the streets they would surround a person, hold him tightly under the arms, and carry him with them against his will.

Money, wine, and hope of plunder fired the zeal of the criminals making up the hoards of brigands described as, "men of rapine and carnage, thirsting for blood and booty." In all of the major uprisings: the siege of the Bastille, the march on Versailles, the invasion of the Tuileries, the massacres of September, and the Reign of Terror, these brigands made up the hard core of the mobs. The bulk of the atrocities that occurred during the Revolution was carried out by these hired assassins. After the first successful uprising, Mirabeau asserted that, "with 100 louis one can make quite a good riot."

To generate an atmosphere of hysteria among the inhabitants of Paris, a constant barrage of false rumors and outright lies emanated from the leaders of the Revolution. Amazing though it was, no matter how outrageous the lies, no matter how many rumors proved to be false, the people never seemed to catch on. This led one observer to state, "Thus it is in revolutions, one rascal writes and a hundred thousand fools believe."

From the very beginning the National Assembly showed no real intention of getting down to the real business of reforms. Every concession upon the part of the King and Nobles was met with a new outbreak of denunciation, outbreaks of violence, and increased demands. It was not reform, but revolution that the conspiracy wanted.

The siege of the Bastille (July 14, 1789) was a brilliant coup of deception upon the part of the revolutionaries. After being terrorized by increasing acts of violence by the brigands, and the breakdown of law and order, the people of Paris sought to obtain arms with which to protect themselves. Rumors were then spread that the Bastille housed the needed arms; whereupon, a large crowd went to the Bastille seeking arms, not only for their own safety, but to defend the Monarchy as well.

What they found in this "hated emblem of despotism," as portrayed by revolutionary writers, were not captives in chains or torture-chambers, but seven prisoners living in relative comfort. Four of the prisoners were forgers, two were lunatics, and one was a man who had been incarcerated at the request of his own family. The King had already planned to tear down the ancient prison, but this was something his enemies could not afford him the honor of doing.

An area also not overlooked by the revolutionaries was the corrupting of the military, whether by bribery, the use of prostitutes, or outright murder. Surprisingly, Lafayette became a member of the Illuminati and joined the Revolution shortly after helping George Washington defeat the British. Lafayette vacillated back and forth between support for the Revolution and support for the Monarchy until he was forced to flee to the frontier where he was arrested and imprisoned by the Austrians.

Because of Lafayette's wavering, the Queen was once quoted as having said, "God save us from being saved by Lafayette."

In the second great uprising of the Revolution, the march on Versailles, October 5 & 6, 1789, the same pattern was used as before. First create a crisis, then on the pretense of solving the crisis, lead the people to action with a hard core of hired revolutionaries. In this case, the manufactured crisis was the hunger caused by agents of the Orleaniste Conspiracy buying up the available grain, and withholding it from the people. The people of Paris were then told that the King and Queen were responsible for the shortage, and that they must march on the King's residence to obtain bread.

As before, besides those who were actually hungry, many of the crowd had been bribed or forced to participate against their will. The women had been placed in the forefront to prevent the soldiers from using arms to disperse the crowd as they advanced. Among the women in the lead were several men dressed in women's clothing to disguise their identity.

Two events prevented the overthrow of the Monarchy on this occasion. One was the bravery of the King in facing the crowd and his magnanimity in offering to give the bread in Versailles to feed the hungry. The other event was the arrival of Lafayette to put down the insurrection.

The one good thing that came out of the march on Versailles was the opening of the eyes of Lafayette to the

Orleaniste Conspiracy. This resulted in public exposure of the conspiracy and the exile of the Duke of Orleans. Unfortunately, this did not put an end to its role in the French Revolution.

After a period of nearly three years the third great outbreak occurred, the siege of the Tuileries on August 10, 1792. This occurred at a time when the Jacobin Clubs literally ruled France. In 1789 the people had chosen their representatives, but due largely to the influence of Robespierre (another member of the Illuminati), those men who had worked out the Constitution of 1791 were not allowed to be members of the new States General.

Referring to the Jacobin Clubs, Dumouriez said:

> This society extending everywhere its numerous affiliations, made use of the provincial clubs to make itself master of the elections. All the cranks, all the seditious scribblers, all the agitators were chosen to go and represent the nation, . . . [6]

By day these representatives of the Jacobin Clubs sat in the Assembly and blocked any real progress toward reforms by endless quibbling over unimportant details. By night they met in secret circles plotting revolution.

As we view the third great uprising, we begin to see the true face of the Revolution with the mask of "reform" ripped away.

One of the lying rumors used to stir the people of Paris into insurrection was that 15,000 aristocrats were ready to massacre all the patriots. The people were then told that, to prevent this planned massacre, the King's residence must be invaded and the Monarchy overthrown. This was the opposite of what was about to happen. It was not the aristocrats who were planning a massacre, it was the revolutionaries. As had happened at Versailles, when the mob invaded the King's residence, he instructed his guards not to fire on the crowd to protect him.

Upon the fall of the Tuileries, the mob went mad in a rage of destruction. Everything in their path was an object of spoliation. Furniture, mirrors, paintings, art work, jewels, all were pillaged or destroyed. Thousands of bottles of wine were taken from the wine cellars and a drunken orgy followed.

The Swiss guards who had remained at their posts were barbarously butchered, including the wounded that lay helpless on the floor. The savage horde tracked down their victims from the deepest cellars to the highest attics. All were put to death.

People danced amid torrents of blood and wine. One man played the violin beside the corpses as the dead bodies were mutilated. Fires were kindled in the apartments and "cutlets of Swiss" were grilled and eaten in cannibal orgies. One man caught up in a fit of revolutionary frenzy, drank a glass of blood.

The power of the conspiracy behind the Revolution was gaining such force that it would not only sweep away King, nobles, and clergy, but eventually, the leaders of the Revolution as well. The end result was a reign of terror and anarchy.

Although sentiment in America over the Revolution was divided, there were several wise and able statesmen who could see the coming holocaust. In his book *Architects of Conspiracy,* William P. Hoar relates the insight of John Adams:

> But the fact is that a number of Americans were skeptical of the French Revolution from its beginning. Among these was the always perceptive John Adams. Biographer Page Smith reports that Adams "from the first moment viewed it with misgivings . . . . At the same time he could not forbear to point out 'that the form of government they have adopted' could be 'nothing more than a transient experiment. An obstinate adherence to it' would involve France 'in great and lasting calamities.' A single assembly would be dominated by demagogues and the result would be repeated upheavals and disorder — a succession of bloody contentions."[7]

Another American statesman who viewed events in France with alarm was Gouverneur Morris. William P. Hoar also recorded Morris' views:

> On the scene as our Minister in Paris was Gouverneur Morris, the conservative statesman who had been the architect of much of the U. S. Constitution.

Morris wrote from France in July of 1789 that "this country is at present as near to anarchy as society can approach without dissolution. . . . The authority of the King and the nobility is completely subdued, but yet I tremble for the constitution."[8]

As the success and power of the conspiracy increased, so did the atrocities, rising to a new level of barbarism during the massacres of September. This period began with the rise to power of the Commune under Marat.

Jean Paul Marat was a native of Switzerland who had spent many years in England studying and practicing medicine. While in England, he attempted to stir up the people against the government by publishing a pamphlet entitled *The Chains of Slavery*. This effort failed and he went to France where he was employed by Danton. Marat (a member of the Illuminati) had one consistent theme in his writings, the abolition of all class distinctions, and the destruction of all who resisted.

In appearance Marat was an aberration of the human race. A dwarf under five feet high, he had a monstrous head, a broken nose, and bronze skin like yellowed parchment. A burning and haggard eye like a hyena added to this, giving him the appearance of something out of this world. He usually wore a ragged coat of faded green, dingy yellow collar, and a dirty handkerchief around his head. "People feared to speak before Marat," says his panegyrist Esquiros; "at the slightest contradiction he shows signs of fury, and if one persisted in one's opinion he flew into a rage and foamed at the mouth."[9]

Following the 10th of August, Marat began to incite the population to massacre the Royalists and Swiss who had been imprisoned. Meeting in secret, Marat and his supporters plotted the details of the massacres of September. For the purpose of robbery, a number of wealthy people were to also be incarcerated. Many of their rivals were added to the list. All of these unfortunate victims were to be imprisoned and put to death without a trial of any kind.

The difficulty in finding enough hands to murder hundreds of prisoners necessitated liberating a number of thieves and murderers from prison. Female malefactors were sometimes released to make up an audience to applaud and incite the murderers to further acts of violence.

Out of well over a thousand victims from nine prisons, the vast majority were from the common people. This list included many young boys, twelve years old and up, who were street urchins detained for minor offenses. At a house of corrections for women, thirty-five victims perished, some being girls ten to fifteen years of age.

Among the victims there were also more than two-hundred priests. These were humble, saintly men, many white haired with age, who had spent their lives in doing good. They met their death with a heroic resignation unsurpassed even by the martyrs of the early church.

Marat blamed the assassinations on the people. Despite the overwhelming evidence to the contrary, historians have attempted to whitewash the role of Marat and his followers by writing that "the people of Paris, overcome by panic, marched to the prisons and massacred the prisoners."[10]

The truth is that the assassins were a group of less than three-hundred men, most of whom were Marseillais and released convicts. A few were middle class tradesmen. The most willing to do the hideous work were men of education. The rest were persuaded by the promise of wine and booty in addition to their salary.

There is evidence that a drug was put in the drink distributed to the assassins. The drug inspired terrible fury and left them without reason. Some witnesses recorded that, because of the drug, most of these assassins died in misery, with an insatiable thirst, and unable to sleep for weeks.

Although many priests perished in the massacres of September (1792), the real work of destroying Christianity in France (Catholic and Protestant alike) did not begin until the 6th of November 1793. The signal for the desecration of the churches and imprisonment of the priests throughout France began with the bishop of Paris (Gobel) being forced to publicly denounce the Catholic religion and declaring that there should be no other worship than that of "liberty and holy equality."

Notre Dame was stripped of its crucifixes and images of the saints and, on November 10, the Feast of Reason took place. Here, Mlle Maillard, an opera singer, believed to be a prostitute, was crowned the "Goddess of Reason."

At the convention an address was presented demanding that:

> Reason and Virtue, should be substituted for the worship of the "Jewish slave" and "the adulterous woman, the courtesan of Galilee."[11]

The person who played the leading part in the campaign against religion was a Prussian baron named Anacharsis Clootz. He was a member of the Illuminati and had declared himself the personal enemy of Jesus Christ. Clootz wrote that, "Religion is a social disease which cannot be too quickly cured. A religious man is a depraved animal; . . ."[12]

By intrigue, Clootz was able to get himself made a Representative of the Nation, and became a major influence in getting the government to sanction the antireligious movement.

Everywhere in France an orgy of blasphemy and desecration began. By order of the government, inscriptions were put up in cemeteries all over France stating that, "Death is an eternal sleep." This was a cherished maxim of the Illuminati and, of course, an official denial of the Resurrection. Not content with destroying the body, the regenerators of France set out to destroy the soul.

Commenting upon the attack against religion and morality during the French Revolution, John Robison stated:

> . . . in all those villainous machinations against the peace of the world, the attack has been first made on the principles of Morality and Religion. The conspirators saw that till these are extripated, they have no chance of success; and their manner of proceeding shews that they consider Religion and Morality as inseparably connected together.[13]

After the death of the King in 1793, the leaders of the Revolution, who now had total control of the government, set out to make terror the order of the day. This terror was not only applied to the common people but to each other as well. Robespierre and his followers, drunk with power, set out to wage war on civilization in the name of Socialism.

Rational for the acts that were to follow was expressed in this manner by Nesta Webster:

> The great criminals of history were not the people inspired by the worst motives, but the people for whom this distinction did not exist . . . the doctrine that has produced all the worst atrocities in the history of the civilized world — namely, that "the end justifies the means" . . . the community or nation which accepts the belief that everything is justifiable — lying, duplicity, treachery, and murder — in order to benefit the cause it has embraced, sells its soul to the devil. To hold this

doctrine is not only to repudiate Christianity, but to strike at the very root of all morality.[14]

In the course of planning for the happiness of the human race, and to transform France into a Socialist State with absolute equality and universal contentment, Robespierre and his followers decided that the population must be reduced by more than half.

This began what was known as the Reign of Terror whereby war was waged against everything that makes up a civilized society. This war, of the government of France against its own people, was as terrible and destructive as any that could have been carried out by an invading army. It was waged with special fury on the manufacturing towns.

The magnificent city of Lyon was literally demolished as orators incited the working-class to violence against the owners of industry. Nor did the war stop with industry, but extended to education, science, art, and literature. Throughout France, thousands of books and valuable pictures were destroyed or sold for next to nothing.

Men of education were subject to arrest and persecution. Even the appearance of culture became dangerous and, in order to survive, it became necessary to dress unkempt and careless and to assume a rough manner. Just to show politeness and good manners placed one in danger of the guillotine.

In order to carry out the government's plan of population control, people were slaughtered by the hundreds and thousands. When the guillotine proved too slow, those rounded up were herded together and blown to pieces by rifle and cannon fire. So great was the slaughter that the Rhone River ran red with the blood of the corpses thrown into it.

Jean Baptiste Carrier had a peculiar hatred against children. "They must be destroyed," he roared, and gave orders that they should be butchered. Under his command at Nantes, 500 children were driven into a field, and then shot, clubbed, and sabered as they clung to the knees of their assassins, weeping and crying for mercy.

It was Carrier who devised the scheme of wholesale drowning in the Loire. The first experiment was made on about ninety old priests who were placed on a barge that was towed to midstream and sunk. Through cold December nights crowds of poor women, some carrying babies, some leading children by the hand, were driven to the river and loaded on barges to be drowned. Carrier referred to this as, "bathing parties." Prudhomme placed the death toll at no less than one million during this period of indiscriminate massacres.

It is important to remember that the system behind the Reign of Terror was the plan of Robespierre to transform France into a Socialist State. There were to be no rich, no poor, only equality. Plans were put forth for every department of life to be placed under State control. Free love was to replace marriage, friendships were to be forced upon people by law, children were to become property of the State, with the State dictating how they should be raised. No area of life was to escape the watchful eye of big brother.

What had all of this done to the people of France? Not only had it destroyed their industries, their commerce, their culture, and their families, its destruction had also reached into the very soul of France. A personal observation of this was told by the British historian John Robison:

> A most worthy and accomplished gentleman, who took refuge in this country, leaving behind him his property, and friends to whom he was most tenderly attached, often said to me that nothing so much affected him as the revolution in the hearts of men. — Characters which were unspotted, hearts thoroughly known to himself, having been tried by many things which search the inmost folds of selfishness or malevolence — in short, persons whose judgements were excellent, and on whose worth he could have rested his honor and his life, so fascinated by the contagion, that they came at last to behold, and even to commit the most atrocious crimes with delight.[15]

And what of the men who planned and carried out the Revolution? Almost to a man they perished as a result of the terror they had created for others. Procession after procession made its way to the guillotine as the factions and leaders turned on and destroyed each other. The lust for blood that they had created, had eliminated all sense of loyalty or justice, even to one another. The list of the victims of their own folly is so long that we will only name a few.

The Duke of Orleans, the man who had pledged his honor, his fortune, and his blood to the revolution, in the end sacrificed them all. Used as a tool, cheated, and ruined by the conspiracy he espoused, he was finally led to the guillotine amid the insults and jeers of the populace of whom he had been represented as an idol.

Mirabeau, an early leader of the Revolution, died suddenly just two days after having turned against his former friends.

Danton, the man who helped plan and carry out the massacres of September, was sentenced to death and executed at the guillotine.

Marat, who had called for the death of so many, was stabbed through the heart by a woman while in his own home. Even after his death an unholy fascination centered around him. Crowds of worshipers knelt around his body, blaspheming Christ and crying out, "Oh sacred heart of Marat!" Added to the display of Satanic admiration was the fact that his body decayed with amazing rapidity immediately after his death.

Carrier, who ordered the murder of innocent children, was executed by the guillotine surrounded by a jeering multitude.

Robespierre, the chief architect of the events from October 1793 on, was the last, and died a hideous death.

Seeing the end near, Robespierre fired a pistol at his head in an attempted suicide, but only succeeded in fracturing his jaw. For hours he lay on a green table, the same table where he and his followers had often sat planning the death of others. As he lay with his head on a wooden box, with blood flowing from his jaw, a workingman approached, looked into the shattered face and exclaimed, "There is a God!"

At the guillotine the executioner tore away the bandage that was bound about his head causing the fractured jaw to fall, leaving a gaping chasm. The victim then emitted a tortured roar of agony that was heard to the farthermost extremities of the square. When his severed head was held up by the executioner, men and women fell into each others arms crying, "At last we are free! The tyrant is no more!" The Reign of Terror had ended.

The end of the Reign of Terror was not the end of turmoil for France. Eighty years of war and revolution were to follow. The Directory (1795-1799) that succeeded the Convention lasted four years and was abolished because of its tyranny and corruption. The Consulate was formed (1799) and ended five years later.

In 1804 Napoleon became emperor and a series of European wars followed resulting in France being invaded by Russians, Austrians, and Prussians. Napoleon was overthrown and France returned to a monarchy in 1814 by calling Louis XVIII to the throne, only to be deposed by Napoleon six months later. Napoleon was defeated at Waterloo, and again foreign armies entered France.

Louis XVIII was recalled and served nine years until his death. His was the only government that did not come to a violent end during the eighty year period. The reign of Charles X that followed was overthrown in 1830 by an uprising of the Orleanists that placed Louis Philippe on the throne, only to be driven out after eighteen years of unrest. In this third revolution of 1848, a Second Republic was proclaimed.

Nesta Webster summed up the whole affair in this manner:

> The immense reforms brought about during the revolutionary era were not the result of the Revolution. It was to the King and his enlightened advisors . . . that the reforms in government were primarily due; it was the *noblesse* that dealt the death-blow to the feudal system; it was the Royalist Democrats, abhorred of the revolutionary leaders, who drew up the Declaration of the Rights of Man and framed the Constitution. The work of the Revolution was to destroy all three reforms — to abolish the liberty of the press, liberty of conscience, personal liberty, to replace the comparatively mild feudalism of the Old Regime by the most frightful tyranny the world has ever seen, and finally to annul the Constitution demanded by the people in favor of a Constitution that could never be enforced, that lasted exactly twenty-six months, and was followed by no less than six others in the eighty years that followed.[16]

Chapter 7

The American Republic

Blessed is the nation whose God is the Lord; . . .
Psalms 33:12

The most amazing thing about the American Republic is that it came into existence. Born into a hostile world, brought to birth by a divided band of colonies, facing one of the most powerful nations on earth determined to destroy it, how could it survive? The answer is, the American Republic almost did not survive.

The Declaration of Independence, the defeat of the British, the writing and ratification of the Constitution, were all events not likely to have happened without the aid of Divine Providence. This is attested to by the actions and expressions of those involved in these events.

The painting of George Washington kneeling in the snow and praying at Valley Forge did not come about as a result of some artist's fancy, but because of the witness of Isaac Potts who, while walking through the woods, accidentally came across Washington praying in a grove of oaks. General Knox, who was with Washington at Valley Forge, stated that Washington frequently used the grove for prayer.

When the Constitutional Convention was on the verge of breaking up, Benjamin Franklin stood up and made a motion stating:

> In the beginning of the contest with Britain, when we were sensible of danger, we had daily prayers in this room for the divine protection. Our prayers, Sir, were heard — and they were graciously answered. . . .
>
> I therefore beg leave to move that, henceforth, prayers imploring the assistance of heaven and its blessings on our deliberations be held in this assembly every morning before we proceed to business, and that one or more of the clergy of this city be requested to officiate in that service.[1]

The record is replete with examples of the Founding Fathers' reliance on, and thankfulness for, Divine assistance.

It may be far more than just a coincidence that the founding of the Illuminati and the founding of the American Republic both took place in 1776. For over a hundred years, the Republic stood as a roadblock to Weishaupt's scheme for his Order to rule the world. During this period, the American Republic was a shining example of everything that was contrary to what the Illuminati and its followers were bringing upon the world. Out of this difference has come a protracted struggle between good and evil, freedom and slavery, which has continued throughout the twentieth century.

To understand better why the Founding Fathers established the kind of government that they did, it is helpful to consider the background of the Founding Fathers themselves, the most common denominator being their Christian Faith. This is not something attributed to them by others, but something established by their own writings and background. Out of the fifty-five delegates to the Constitutional Convention, Christianity was the religion of at least fifty. This means that 90 percent of the delegates were Christians. For an excellent 415 page book covering this subject, we recommend *Christianity And The Constitution* by John Eidsmoe published by Baker Book House, Grand Rapids, Michigan. To learn the truth about the beliefs of the Founding Fathers, Eidsmoe personally read 5,000 letters written by these men.

Not only were the Founding Fathers well versed in Scripture, they were also well educated in history. One thing that made the founding of the American Republic possible was the high rate of literacy and high standard of education among the colonists. Eidsmoe gives us an idea of this level:

> The high caliber of learning at that time is evident from the entrance requirements for colonial colleges. In the 1700s an undergraduate freshman at William and Mary College had to be able to read, write, converse, and debate in Greek. When John Jay applied for admission to King's College in New York at the age of fourteen, one of the entrance requirements he had to fulfill was to translate the first ten chapters of the Gospel of John from Greek into Latin.[2]

Around 1800 a study was made on education in America that concluded, "Most young Americans . . . can read, write and cipher. Not more than four in a thousand are unable to write legibly — even neatly."[3]

This high rate of literacy was a direct result of the religious leaders placing a strong emphasis upon the importance of being able to read the Bible. There were no public schools at this time.

Because of their knowledge of history, secular and religious, the Founding Fathers had a profound faith in Divine Providence and a strong distrust in government. Thus, they set out to establish a system of government that would set men free to work out their own destiny by binding rulers down "with the chains of the Constitution."

The United States Constitution was not something hammered out over night, but was carefully written after much consideration and debate. The war with Britain ended on October 19, 1781, but the Constitution was not ratified until June 1788. Two years later, December 1791, the Bill of Rights was adopted.

To understand better the events leading up to the founding of the American Republic, and why the Founding Fathers gave us the kind of government they did, it will be helpful to examine the Old World View of man and government.

This view was largely a fatalistic view that the individual is helpless to determine his destiny, that he is controlled by forces outside himself and can do nothing to improve his lot in life. Therefore, he needed a king or leader to guide and control him. In this stagnant world, with no hope of progress, men must be herded into a collective mass, a bee hive, and controlled.

This pagan view was dominant for nearly 6,000 years of recorded history with the result that hunger and famine remained a common foe for most of the inhabitants of earth. Progress was so slow that, until the time of George Washington, the best thing that man could come up with for transportation was the horse drawn coach, and that could only be afforded by the rich. Then something amazing happened. The Old World pagan concepts were rejected, resulting in more progress toward a better way of life in less than 200 years than the accumulated progress of 6,000 years.

The events leading up to this quantum leap forward actually began on the American Continent as far back as 1660. It was during this time that the colonies began to rebel against the pagan Old World View of a planned economy.

Charles II had signed an act allowing the American Colonies to ship cotton, lumber, tobacco, and other products to England, but only to England, nowhere else. The colonists needed sugar and molasses from the West Indies (Cuba). Therefore, they just ignored the King's decree and kept on trading wool and tobacco for sugar and molasses. A few of the traders' ships were sunk by the King's navy, but this was just considered an ordinary business risk.

In 1760 King George III came along and set out to control every detail affecting the lives of his subjects at home and abroad. The first thing he did was restrict emigration to the colonies and prohibit any more settlers from moving westward. The King's planning even included American trees, with the King's men going through the forest and marking the best pine to be held for the royal navy.

This so irritated the colonists that they not only went out of their way to use the marked trees, they also adopted the pine tree as their symbol of liberty. Whenever the British government tried to place restrictions on trade, the colonists went right on trading. When the weaving of cloth was prohibited in the colonies, the women went right on working at their looms, with the stage being set for a confrontation until finally, "the embattled farmers" stood at the Concord bridge and fired the "the shot heard 'round the world."

It is interesting to note, that in trying to manage a planned economy, the object of government regulations is always to prevent a fall in prices, just the opposite of what creates prosperity. What government has never learned is that lower prices, not higher prices, aid the economy. It is an unheeded lesson of history that government interference in the marketplace always works to harmful ends. It never helps.

Henry Grady Weaver in his book, *The Mainspring of Human Progress,* explained how this brought down the Roman Empire:

> The hairsplitting economic regulations were perfected by Diocletian, whose stern directives were so efficiently administered that farmers could no longer farm; and many of the small businessmen, faced with starvation, committed suicide in preference to being executed for black marketing.[4]

When there was no work, the beneficent government then began to tax the rich to provide the populace with bread and entertainment. Eventually, so many workers were forced into tax-supported relief that there was not enough production to pay the tax bills. The result; the Roman Empire collapsed into the dark ages.

In England, to solve the problem of over production of wool, Charles II decreed that no corpse could be buried that was not wrapped in a woolen shroud. The wool was buried, but ghouls dug up the corpses, stole the shrouds and sold them on the black market. Before Adam Smith's *Wealth of Nations* was published (in 1776), and his ideas made the Industrial Revolution possible, England was known as an island surrounded by smugglers.

Weaver also quoted Buckle's comments on France:

> In every quarter, and at every moment, the hand of government was felt. Duties on importation, and duties

on exportation; bounties to raise up a losing trade, and taxes to pull down a remunerative one; this branch of industry forbidden, and that branch of industry encouraged; one article of commerce must not be grown, because it was grown in the colonies, another article might be grown and bought, but not sold again, while a third article might be bought and sold, but not leave the country. Then, too, we find laws to regulate wages; laws to regulate prices; laws to regulate profits; laws to regulate the interest of money; custom-house arrangements of the most vexatious kind, aided by a complicated scheme, which was called the sliding scale, — a scheme of such perverse ingenuity, that the duties constantly varied on the same article, and no man could calculate beforehand what he would have to pay. . . . The tolls were so onerous, as to double and often quadruple the cost of production.[5]

Under the care of the state, planning for their welfare, conditions were such that only smuggling kept the French people from starving to death. The American Colonists knew about planned economy. They wanted none of it.

When the members of the Continental Congress were finally able to get down to the business of establishing the new government, they had a clean slate. The problem was what to write on that slate. Probably no one knew that they would eventually produce what would be heralded as one of the greatest documents ever penned by mortal men — The United States Constitution.

The Constitution was the outcome of the basic philosophy already expressed in the Declaration of Independence:

> We hold these Truths to be self-evident, that all Men are created equal, that they are endowed by their Creator with certain unalienable Rights, that among these are Life, Liberty, and the Pursuit of Happiness. That to secure these Rights, Governments are instituted among Men, deriving their just Powers from the Consent of the Governed.

Never before in the history of mankind had a government been established upon the idea that man's rights came from God and that government's role was to protect those rights that had already been given him by his Creator. Furthermore, under this system, man could work out his own destiny. This was a total rejection of Old World Views of man and government. This was revolutionary!

At this time in history most of the nations were ruled by a monarch. The Founding Fathers rejected this concept of government, and for good reason. Being students of and holding reverence for the Bible, they were familiar with the experience of the Jewish nation of Israel regarding a king. The Law of Moses made no provision for a king. The Israelites were to be ruled by God as responsible individuals, but they wanted to be like other nations, and have a king to rule over them. The Old Testament Scripture records that the leaders of Israel came to the Prophet Samuel and said, ". . . make us a king to judge us like all the nations" I Samuel 8:5. The rest of the story is recorded in I Samuel chapter eight:

> 7 And the Lord said unto Samuel, Hearken unto the voice of the people in all that they say unto thee: for they have not rejected thee, but they have rejected me, that I should not reign over them.
>
> 11 And he said, This will be the manner of the king that shall reign over you: He will take your sons, and appoint them for himself, for his chariots, and to be his horsemen; and some shall run before his chariots.
>
> 12 And he will appoint him captains over thousands, and captains over fifties; and will set them to ear his ground, and to reap his harvest, and to make his instruments of war, and instruments of his chariots.
>
> 13 And he will take your daughters to be confectioneries, and to be cooks, and to be bakers.
>
> 14 And he will take your fields, and your vineyards, and your oliveyards, even the best of them, and give them to his servants.
>
> 15 And he will take the tenth of your seed, and of your vineyards, and give to his officers, and to his servants.
>
> 16 And he will take your menservants, and your maidservants, and your goodliest young men, and your asses, and put them to his work.
>
> 17 He will take the tenth of your sheep: and ye shall be his servants.

Unwilling to accept responsibility, the Israelites rejected the first of the Ten Commandments, "Thou shalt have none other gods before me" in the hope that a king would do for them what they should do for themselves. They rejected a government of fixed laws, for a government based upon the whims of a monarch, the tragic results of which are recorded in the books of the Old Testament.

Another system of government the Founding Fathers rejected was a Democracy. To understand why they rejected a Democracy, we will let them speak for themselves.

On June 21, 1788, Alexander Hamilton made a speech in which he stated:

> It had been observed that a pure democracy if it were practicable would be the most perfect government. Experience has proved that no position is more false than this. The ancient democracies in which the people themselves deliberated never possessed one good feature of government. Their very character was tyranny; their figure deformity.[6]

Samuel Adams warned:

> Remember, Democracy never lasts long. It soon wastes, exhaust and murders itself! There never was a democracy that 'did not commit suicide.'[7]

James Madison wrote:

> . . . . democracies have ever been spectacles of turbulence and contention; have ever been found incompatible with personal security, or the rights of

property; and have in general been as short in their lives as they have been violent in their deaths.[8]

But, why doesn't democracy work? Why isn't it a good form of government? The answer lies in a fatal tendency of man to aspire to live off the labors of someone else. To live, man must either work or steal. Experience shows that he will do whichever is safest and easiest. Thus, the majority will always follow demagogues who promise to use the law to give them other men's property, property usually taken by taxes. Once the law is perverted into a system of legalized plunder to redistribute wealth, a right sense of justice is destroyed. Special interest groups are then formed to lobby government for their share of the wealth. Class hatred is generated, violence and anarchy then usher in the fall of the government and the establishment of a dictatorship.

This process is explained very well in the 1928 U. S. Army Training Manual as it gives a definition of democracy:

A government of the masses. Authority derived through mass meeting or any form of direct expression. Results in mobocracy. Attitude toward property is communistic — negating property rights. Attitude toward law is that the will of the majority shall regulate, whether it be based upon deliberation or governed by passion, prejudice, and impulse, without restraint or regard to consequences. Results in demagogism, license, agitation, discontent, anarchy.[9]

Because of a willingness to profit from the lessons of history, the Founding Fathers adopted a constitution that nowhere mentioned a democracy, as neither did the Declaration of Independence, nor a single constitution of our fifty states.

What the Founding Fathers did choose to establish was a government of written and permanent law. Realizing that men can only remain free by limiting political power, these laws restricted the power of government.

Rather than enumerate a long list of freedoms guaranteed to the people, they enumerated a short list of what government could and could not do. Basically, this limited government to protecting life, liberty, and property.

To guard against usurpation of power, they divided the power between three branches of the federal government, the states, and the people. What the Founding Fathers gave us was a Constitutional Republic.

One of the most important provisions of the Constitution was the establishment of a sound monetary system based upon gold and silver. This too had its roots in Old Testament Bible History. The first metal mentioned in Old Testament Scripture was gold, Genesis 2:11. The location given was near Ancient Babylon, which may have been the reason for it having been referred to as "the golden city," Isaiah 14:4.

The second metal mentioned in Scripture is in reference to Abram (Abraham). It is found in Genesis 13:2, "and Abram was very rich in cattle, in silver, and in gold."

That these two metals were placed in the earth by the Creator shows His infinite wisdom in providing man a basis for a universal monetary system. The creation of gold and silver was one of God's great masterpieces that enabled man to develop a system of commerce in a civilized society.

The use of gold and silver as money did not come about as the result of any government decree or even of Divine commandment. It came about as a result of the choice (often by trial and error) of the people themselves. This choice was made for several reasons.

Gold and silver are universally desired as objects of beauty, especially in the form of jewelry. They are durable, even when lying in the ground for thousands of years. They are divisible, and can be formed into any size or shape. They are also scarce and cannot be produced by any process known to man. These characteristics make gold and silver an ideal store of wealth, which is what real money is.

The Founding Fathers of the American Republic understood the basis of real money, thus, in the Constitution it is spelled out that, "No State shall . . . make anything but gold and silver coin a tender in payment of debts; . . . " Article I, Section 10. The Constitution authorizes the Federal Government to "coin money" Article I, Section 8, but nowhere does it authorize the printing of money. The paper bills originally used in the United States were not recognized as money but were receipts for money and could be redeemed in silver or gold at any time.

This kind of sound money helped to make the United States one of the greatest nations in the world. It also made it impossible for any central power to control the American people and herd them into a one world government. No doubt, this was one of the reasons that subversive forces went to work to destroy this element of American independence.

For a deeper understanding of the importance of a sound monetary system, and why we must return to a sound system, we recommend John F. McManus' book *Financial Terrorism:Hijacking America Under the Threat of Bankruptcy.* It is available from Western Islands, P.O. Box 8040, Appleton, Wisconsin.

Chapter 8

Attempts to Divide America

And if a kingdom be divided against itself, that kingdom cannot stand.

Mark 3:24

Although the establishment of a Constitutional Republic was a great victory for the American people, the struggle for freedom was not over; for, hardly had the ink dried on the Constitution before subversive forces, led by the Illuminati, set out to destroy the new Republic.

It is an interesting coincidence that the first major uprising of the French Revolution, and the first meeting of the new United States Congress, both occurred in the spring of 1789. The same conspiracy that engineered the French Revolution, and the turmoil that kept France in chaos for over 80 years afterward, also jeopardized the new American Republic.

Although, by the beginning of 1800, the Illuminati had set up, or taken control of, some lodges in America, they were never able to accomplish what they had done in France. The main reason for this was that, by 1800, most of the literate people in the United States knew about the Illuminati. This was partly due to the wide distribution of

John Robison's book *Proofs of a Conspiracy* from 1797 to 1798.

Another influential writer who did much to expose the activities of the Illuminati in the United States was Jedediah Morse, the father of Samuel Morse, the famous inventor of the telegraph. Besides many other voices that raised a cry of alarm, George Washington spoke out publicly against their efforts to foment revolution.

I n western Pennsylvania in 1794, a serious insurrection was promoted by a group established by Edmond Charles Genet, an Illuminist, and the French envoy to the United States. This group, known as the Mino Creek Democratic Society, tried to bring about secession and set up a separate country in that region. This event is referred to by historians as the Whiskey Rebellion.

At a cost of a million dollars, President Washington put down the rebellion and publicly denounced the influence of French Illuminists behind it. William P. Hoar said this about the event:

> President Washington believed the revolutionary Democratic Clubs were responsible for the so-called Whiskey Rebellion. Whatever the case, it was certainly the spirit of the French Revolution that sustained it. Albert Beveridge comments that "when the troops sent out to put down insurrection reached Harrisburg, they found the French flag flying over the courthouse." President Washington said: "I consider this insurrection as the first *formidable* fruit of the Democratic Societies

. . . instituted by *artful and designing* members [of Congress] . . . . I see, under a display of popular and fascinating guises, the most diabolical attempts to destroy . . . the government." He further declared: "That they have been the fomenters of the western disturbance admits of no doubt." If "the daring and factious spirit" is not crushed, "adieu to all government in this country, except mob and club government."[1]

When Genet was recalled as French envoy, he never returned to France, but went to live in New York where he carried on his revolutionary activities. He was replaced by M. Fauchet, another roving ambassador for the Illuminati.

Just how dangerous revolutionary activity was to the United States government became known with the accidental discovery of secret communications of M. Fauchet to his superiors in France. Through these dispatches, Washington learned that a member of his own Cabinet, Edmund Randolph, was in league with French revolutionaries. This disclosure led to the resignation of Randolph.

During the next five years a growing number of inflammatory journals calling for a French Revolution in America led to the Alien and Sedition Acts of 1798 as a means to deter threats of violence.

A prominent individual to come out of one of the Illuminist lodges, the Columbian Lodge in New York, was Aaron Burr, the man who shot Alexander Hamilton. From 1801 to 1803 Aaron Burr actively organized revolutionary forces and formed military encampments of private troops up and down the Mississippi River, which was then the western boundary of the United States. His plan was to start an insurrection and break away that portion of the country. Burr's activities came at about the time of the Louisiana Purchase which means that he was making a grab for an immense amount of territory. Aaron Burr was eventually arrested and put on trial.

The Theistical Society was another subversive group that operated out of New York. It's existence was discovered and publicized by John Wood, a Scottish cartographer and teacher. The head of the organization was Elihu Palmer a blind minister. Palmer was a deist who denied the existence of a personal God. William H. McIlhany said this about the Society:

> Like its Bavarian origin, the Society promoted the distribution of publications attacking all religious belief and any form of government other than democracy. Most notable among these, in addition to Paine's *Age of Reason,* was Palmer's own *Principles of Nature.*[2]

Theistical Society members advocated using a strategy of "patient gradualism" to accomplish their goals. They also sought to finance and lead their own opposition in waging a public ideological crusade against them. This was done to give the Society the appearance of nothing more than the promoter of an idealistic campaign, thus obscuring their secret subversive program. This program, of leading your opposition, has been used with great success by other subversive organizations throughout the the 20th century.

William P. Hoar had this to say about the early internal attacks against America:

> The young and independent Republic of the United States had survived subversion by a European conspiracy and now had breathing space in which to recuperate. The disease, however, had not been conquered and would appear again.[3]

In spite of tremendous odds, America fulfilled her destiny and survived to become the world's greatest example of what men can accomplish when free from the life-choking restraints of Socialism. By the beginning of the the century, the United States was one of the wealthiest and most powerful nations on earth.

Religious freedom enabled Americans to build more churches, establish more schools, publish more Bibles, and send more missionaries than any other country had yet been able to do.

American greatness continued right up to the beginning of the 20th century when more and more people began to forget the warnings expressed by men like William Cullen Bryant, "Not yet, O freedom! Close thy lids in slumber, for thine enemy never sleeps."

Chapter 9

Mystery Babylon Unveiled

> And upon her forehead was a name written, MYSTERY, BABYLON THE GREAT, THE MOTHER OF HARLOTS AND ABOMINATIONS OF THE EARTH.
>
> Revelation 17:5

> And the angel said unto me, Wherefore didst thou marvel? I will tell thee the mystery of the woman, . . .
>
> Revelation 17:7

Although many events pictured in the book of Revelation are veiled in mystery, the veil of mystery is lifted from Mystery Babylon. The Apostle John records that after seeing a vision of an outwardly beautiful woman identified as Mystery, Babylon The Great, he is then told that the mystery of the woman will be explained. This explanation then follows, beginning with Revelation 17:18 and continuing for the next twenty-six verses. These verses describe the power, wealth, character, and deeds of the men who make up Babylon.

Babylon's seat of power is described as a "great city" six times. It is not described as a nation or kingdom but as, "that great city, which reigneth over the kings of the earth."

Eight references are made to Babylon as a center of world commerce, much of it by maritime trade. It is described as, "that great city, wherein were made rich all that had ships in the sea by reason of her costliness" Revelation 18:19.

The men of Babylon are described as merchants who are men of renown, "for thy merchants were the great men of the earth;" Revelation 18:23. Twenty-five items of their commerce are listed. Many items are such as could only be afforded by the rich. Slaves are included in this list found in Revelation 18:12 & 13.

Although the men of Babylon are described as outwardly powerful and wealthy businessmen, inwardly, they are described in some of the harshest terms found in Scripture. Four times the word "whore" is used and five times the word "fornication" is used.

Whenever these terms were used in Old Testament Scripture, in reference to rulers or nations, they always referred to idolatry. For example, Ezekiel condemned the worship of Molech (an Ammonite god) by the nation of Judah in these terms, "Moreover thou hast taken thy sons and daughters, whom thou hast borne unto me, and these hast thou sacrificed unto them to be devoured. Is this thy whoredoms a small matter," Ezekiel 16:20. This idolatrous practice of human sacrifice was referred to as "whoredoms." The word "fornication" was also used to describe idolatry, "Thou hast also committed fornication with the Egyptians thy neighbors," Ezekiel 16:26. The description of Mystery Babylon that John gave in

Revelation 19:2 as, "the great whore, which did corrupt the earth with her fornication," signifies universal idolatry.

This would indicate that Mystery Babylon will be a world leader in a return to a pagan worship of nature that denies God as creator, exactly as we see in the New Age Movement. More than any other single evil, it was idolatry that led to the downfall of the nation of Israel. The Bible condemns idolatry as evil because, it not only denies God as creator, and regards man on the level of animals, it often leads to the shedding of the blood of innocent human beings.

Babylon's leaders were condemned for using sorceries (the assistance of evil spirits) to deceive the nations, "for by thy sorceries were all nations deceived" Revelation 18:23.

Babylon is also described as the instigator of mass murder with a Satanic hatred of those who believe in God. "And in her was found the blood of prophets, and of saints, and of all that were slain upon the earth" Revelation 18:24. The Apostle John gave this witness in Revelation 17:6, "And I saw the woman drunken with the blood of the saints, and with the blood of the martyrs of Jesus: . . ."

The picture of Mystery Babylon is so terrible that the first mention of it in Revelation 14:8 gives the good news first, "And there followed another angel, saying, Babylon is fallen, is fallen, that great city, because she made all the nations drink of the wine of the wrath of her fornication." The fall of Babylon is also mentioned in at least seven verses in the 17th and 18th chapters of Revelation.

As we examine events on the secret side of history during the 20th century, our readers can decide for themselves whether or not the pattern of these events fits Mystery Babylon. They can also decide if this pattern matches the program laid down by Adam Weishaupt to destroy all religion, overthrow all governments, and rule the world.

Chapter 10

Building Modern Babylon

Alas, alas, that great city, that was clothed in fine linen, and purple, and scarlet, and decked with gold, and precious stones, and pearls!
Revelation 18:16

. . . for thy merchants were the great men of the earth; for by thy sorceries were all nations deceived.
Revelation 18:23

At the beginning of the 20th century, in New York, there began an association known as the "Money Trust." This came about because of a combining of European and United States banking interests, and was centered around powerful American money barons such as J. P. Morgan, John D. Rockefeller, and Bernard Baruch. One of America's most powerful banking firms, Kuhn, Loeb and Company, with ties to the Rothschilds' European banking dynasty, was also involved.

In 1902, Paul Warburg (a German banker associated with the Rothschilds) came to the United States and was paid a $500,000 yearly salary while campaigning for the establishment of a central banking system. This system was patterned after the European system where the

Rothschilds owned the Bank of England, the Bank of France, and the Bank of Germany.

To accomplish their goal of establishing a central bank, the Money Trust used a proven method of revolution, that of creating a crisis and then offering a solution, the solution being what the perpetrators wanted in the first place.

In this case, the crisis was the Bank Panic of 1907. It was created by J. P. Morgan spreading the rumor that the Trust Company of America (a private bank) was insolvent. This resulted in snowballing bank runs. The Money Trust then came forward with a solution to prevent bank runs, a central bank to control all banking in the United States.

Plans for a central bank were formalized, in 1910, in a secret meeting at J. P. Morgan's hunting club on Jekyll Island, off the coast of Georgia. At this meeting, along with representatives of the Money Trust, was Senator Nelson Aldrich, a relative of the Rockefellers. Aldrich became the chief proponent of legislation in Congress to create a central bank. In December of 1913, Congress passed legislation creating the Federal Reserve. The United States had a central bank.

Another time worn method was used by the conspirators to get the American people to accept a central bank. This method is always to promise just the opposite of what you intend to do. The Federal Reserve was sold to Congress as a way to stabilize the economy and prevent future bank runs. It did just the opposite. It was the action, and then the inaction, of the Federal Reserve that helped cause, and prolong, the Great Depression of 1929. It is often overlooked that the Great Depression of 1929 came sixteen years after the Federal Reserve was supposedly created to prevent just such an occurrence. The truth is, without the Federal Reserve, it would not have happened.

Congressman Charles Lindbergh (father of the famous aviator Charles Lindberg) referred to the Federal Reserve as, "the invisible government by the money powers." He also stated, "This act establishes the most gigantic trust on earth. . . ."[1]

Congressman Louis McFadden, chairman of the House Committee on Banking and Currency from 1920 to 1931, later declared:

> When the Federal Reserve Act was passed, the people of these United States did not perceive that a world banking system was being set up here.
>
> A super-state controlled by international bankers and international industrialists acting together to enslave the world for their own pleasure.[2]

This system, referred to by Congressman McFadden, is a privately owned banking system. Although its name, the Federal Reserve, implies that it is government owned and controlled, it is so powerful that not even Congress has ever been able to have it audited, nor does anyone outside its banking circles know who owns the bank.

In the same year the Federal Reserve came into being, the Federal Income Tax also became law. It was sold to the American people with the inference that it would never be increased above the original 1 percent of income. The chief proponent of this legislation in Congress was also Senator Nelson Aldrich.

Another important consideration for the members of the Money Trust was the establishment of tax-free foundations, whereby their own wealth would be sheltered from the income tax, and still be under their control. This was accomplished before the passage of the income tax.

With the establishment of the Federal Reserve, private bankers had several means to control and use the money system of the United States, not only to accumulate great wealth for themselves, but also to extend the power of the Federal Government over the nation as a whole and over the people as individuals. One method repeatedly used has been the creation of "booms and busts" in the economy, with those at the top knowing ahead of time what to expect of the money market.

It is argued that the men who control the Federal Reserve are above using their power for personal gain. This argument raises two important questions. The first question is, if that is the case, Why do they want this power? The second is, Why have they used this power repeatedly over a period of a century? For, it can be proven, that most of the booms and busts in the economy came "after" an action by the Federal Reserve, not before. In other words, The Federal Reserve has been manipulating the American economy for nearly a century.

Another method of accumulating great wealth is through lending the government money created out of nothing more than a bookkeeping entry, and then earning interest on this money. A feature of this system is that the introduction of unbacked money actually serves as a hidden tax by decreasing the buying power of all the money in circulation.

This method (inflation of the money supply) has been used to the extent that $10,000 in 1940 now has the buying power of only $500. By 1971 all ties of gold or silver to our paper currency had been eliminated, making it possible to inflate it to worthlessness, as was done in Germany prior to the rise of Hitler.

Once the Federal Reserve had the power to lend vast amounts of money to the government, and the income tax had been established as a way to collect the money to pay the interest on the loans, the United States was on its way to becoming one of the worlds largest debtor nations.

This debt is increasing at the rate of a billion dollars a day. As a result a gigantic crisis is being created to lead us into a one world monetary system under the control of the same people who created the problem.

The president of American Media, G. Edward Griffin, gave this possible scenario regarding inflation:

When inflation really becomes rampant, when it gets to the point where people literally have to rush to the grocery stores with their paychecks in order to buy food, because if they wait until the next day the price will have gone up on a loaf of bread, and their paycheck will no longer be as valuable 24 hours later, when it gets to the point where people are having their savings literally wiped out because the value of the money that they have in savings is falling so rapidly, then it's important for the government to have to do something to supposedly cure this problem. Well, the fact of the matter is, the government is the culprit, or the entity that created the problem in the first place.

I think somewhere down the line when inflation heats up here in the United States, and it becomes more obvious that it is something of concern, the government will be expected to do something about it, and one of the things they will probably do is issue a new currency . . .

The most important function to be served by the new monetary unit, or this new currency we are talking about, is a transition to a true world monetary unit, or a world currency.

The bottom line of all this, is that we are headed, if we don't do something about it, directly into a one world government. One of the most obvious evidences of a one world government is a one world monetary unit.[3]

As a solution to this manufactured crisis Mr. Griffin had this to say:

Nothing is going to happen in the realm of political change unless Congress makes it happen. Congress is the body that makes the rules. So nothing is going to change

> — this drift is going to continue. It's going to continue
> unless Congress changes it, and that means Congress has
> to be changed. What we're talking about is virtually a
> revolution in the awareness of the American people.[4]

For a deeper understanding of the conspiratorial forces behind the creation of the Federal Reserve, we recommend G. Edward Griffin's book *The Creature From Jekyll Island . . . A Second Look at the Federal Reserve.* It is available from, American Media, P. O. Box 4646, Westlake Village, California.

The great question is, How has it happened that the American people now find themselves on the verge of losing their independence, and freedom, to a one world government? To answer this question we must examine a chronology of events occurring on the secret side of history during the 20th century.

In 1954 the United States Congress created a special committee to investigate tax-free foundations. This committee was known as the Reece Committee, in recognition of its chairman, Congressman Carroll Reece of Tennessee.

In 1982, G. Edward Griffin interviewed Norman Dodd, staff director of the Reece Committee. Here, in Norman Dodd's own words, is some of the shocking information discovered in the minutes of the Carnegie Endowment for International Peace:

> We are at the year 1908, which was the year that the
> Carnegie began operations, and in that year, the trustees,

meeting for the first time, raised a specific question, which they discussed throughout the balance of the year in a very learned fashion. And the question is, Is there any means known more effective than war, assuming you wish to alter the life of an entire people? They conclude that no more effective means than war, to that end, is known to humanity.

So then, in 1909, they raised the second question and discuss it. Namely, How do we involve the United States in a war? . . . Then finally they answer that question as follows, "We must control the State Department." And then that very naturally raises the question of how to do that. They answer it by saying we must take over and control the diplomatic machinery of this country, and finally they resolve to aim at that as an objective.

Then time passes and we are eventually in a war, which would have been World War I. And at that time they record on their minutes a shocking report in which they dispatch to President Wilson a telegram cautioning him to see that the war does not end too quickly.

And finally, of course, the war is over. At that time their interest shifts over to preventing what they call a reversion of life in the United States to what it was prior to 1914, when World War I broke out. And they, at that point, come to the conclusion that to prevent a reversion we must control education in the United States.[5]

Mr. Dodd then went on to explain the method outlined whereby the grant-making power of the tax-free foundations were to be used to change the teaching of history in the United States.

Even then (1954) subversive forces were so strong that the Reece Committee was unable to complete its investigation and bring this information to the American people. The full one hour interview of Norman Dodd on video tape is available from, American Media, P. O. Box 4646, Westlake Village, California.

To understand why such goals were pursued by the trustees of the Carnegie Endowment for International Peace, it is helpful to understand the background of Andrew Carnegie. Born in Scotland, into a family of radical ideas, he came to the United States with his parents in 1848. Here he rose from a $1.20 per week bobbin-boy to become one of the richest men in the world.

With the right connections during the Civil War, he emerged at the end of that conflict well established in business. A master at dealing in government contracts, he was able to build an empire in the steel industry, selling his interests in 1901 for $250 million.

When public resistance grew against his manipulation of government for profit, Carnegie learned that the best way to overcome a tarnished image was to spend millions of dollars to establish a well-advertised reputation for philanthropy.

Andrew Carnegie was one of the first people in America to call for a "League of Nations" and an international "peace army," in other words, one world government. Throughout his career, he worked with other prominent Americans toward the accomplishment of this goal. Although he made his vast fortune in the United States, he never became an American citizen.

One of the ways the conspirators were able to get the United States into World War I was by getting their man, Woodrow Wilson, into the White House. Wilson was elevated from his position as president of Princeton University to governor of New Jersey. After agreeing to follow certain principles, should he be elected, Wilson was backed for President by the Money Trust. One of the principles Wilson agreed upon was to listen to the advice of the Money Trust should war break out in Europe. He became a close friend of Andrew Carnegie who wrote to him on Feb. 14, 1917, urging that he go ahead with world war for world peace.

At this time the American people had no interest in getting involved in a European war. Wilson even ran for his second term on the slogan "he kept us out of war." Once back in the White House, he began to push for United States entry into World War I. Two outspoken opponents of United States involvement in the war were Henry Ford and Charles A. Lindbergh Sr.

To get the United Sates to declare war on Germany, Wilson contrived with Winston Churchill for the sinking of the Lusitania. This was accomplished by using the Lusitania as a munitions ship. Prior to being sunk, it was sent into U-boat infested waters carrying six million rounds of ammunition, ordered to reduce speed, and deserted by its escort. Hit by a single torpedo, it sank in eighteen minutes due to internal explosions. This information was later revealed by Commander Joseph Kenworthy, who was, at the time, a member of British

Naval Intelligence. Much of the truth about the sinking of the Lusitania was revealed by British author, Colin Simpson, in his book *The Lusitania.*

The deaths of 128 Americans aboard the ill-fated ship propelled the United States into the war. This was despite the fact that Germany had put advertisements in New York newspapers advising Americans not to board the ship because it was carrying munitions to England. To cover up this fact, President Wilson ordered the cargo records listing the munitions sealed up in the national archives. Thus, world events were set into motion, by a master plan of deception, which were eventually to alter the course of history.

The purpose of getting the United States into World War I was to establish world government through the League of Nations. When Congress refused to go along with this scheme, and rejected membership in the League of Nations, it was decided that America would have to be changed before it would enter into world government.

In 1919, at a meeting in Paris led by Colonel Edward Mandel House, it was resolved that an "Institute of International Affairs" be formed with two branches, one in England and one in the United States. The American branch was incorporated in New York as the Council on Foreign Relations on July 29, 1921.

In 1912, a novel was published that had been written by Edward Mandel House. This novel, entitled *Philip Dru: Administrator,* called for "Socialism as dreamed of by Karl Marx." Unfortunately, House lived to see some of this dream come true for the United States.

The organization that House founded, the Council on Foreign Relations (CFR), was to become the hidden government of the United States. From its original membership list of 210 men, the Council on Foreign Relations has grown to include 3,000 of the most prominent leaders in America. For decades it has controlled United States foreign policy and has operated on the secret side of history, shielded from public view.

To guard against exposure, and to mold public opinion, as far back as 1915 the powerful men in America working for world government set out to control the news media. They accomplished this by employing 12 leading men in the newspaper field to find out what was necessary to control the general policy of the daily press throughout the country. It was decided that this could be accomplished by purchasing control of 25 of the greatest papers. Thus, while the Council on Foreign Relations was working to remake the world, for the first 35 years of its existence, no feature article about it appeared in the news media. It was not until the 1960s that this near total control of the media began to be circumvented.

For decades many top officials of the United States Government have been members of the Council on Foreign Relations. This includes many presidents, fourteen secretaries of state, fourteen treasury secretaries, eleven defense secretaries, and scores of other federal department heads.

If any one were to search behind the scenes for an identifiable organization that has worked to establish a Modern Day Babylon, it would be difficult to locate one more important than the Council on Foreign Relations headquartered in the Harold Pratt House, at 58 East 68th Street, in New York City. Former FBI Agent, Dan Smoot, labeled it, *"The Invisible Government."*

In 1954 Norman Dodd met with CFR member Rowan Gaither who was at that time head of the Ford Foundation. This is Mr. Dodd's report of their conversation during that meeting:

Mr. Gaither said, "Mr. Dodd, we have asked you to come up here today because we thought that possibly, off the record, you would tell us why the Congress is interested in the activities of Foundations such as ourselves." And before I could think of how I would reply to that statement, Mr. Gaither then went on voluntarily and stated, "Mr. Dodd all of us that have a hand in making policies here have had experience either with the OSS during the war, or the European Economic Administration. After the war we have had experience operating under directives, and these directives emanate, and did emanate from the White House. Now we still operate under just such directives. Would you like to know what the substance of these directives is?" I said, 'Mr. Gaither, I'd like very much to know.' Whereupon he made this statement to me, namely, "Mr. Dodd, we here operate in response to similar directives, the substance of which is that we shall use our grant making powers so to alter life in the United States that it can be comfortably merged with the Soviet Union."[6]

When Norman Dodd asked Rowan Gaither if he would be willing to tell this to the American people he responded that, "This we would not think of doing." To this day that objective of merging the United States with the Soviet Union has not been abandoned.

Many of the 210 men who became original members of the Council on Foreign Relations were supporters of the Bolshevik Revolution in Russia in 1917. It was support from these wealthy businessmen in the United States that helped make the revolution successful.

Jacob Schiff, head of the New York based Kuhn, Loeb and Co., spent $20 million on the revolution. Federal Reserve Director, William Boyce Thompson, gave the Bolsheviks $1 million. In the summer of 1917, fifteen Wall Street financiers and attorneys, led by Thompson, went to Petrograd, the center of revolutionary activity. This was disguised as a Red Cross Mission by taking along a few doctors and nurses. Disillusioned, the doctors and nurses returned home within a month; the financiers stayed from June to November.

After the Revolution in Russia was successful, many American businessmen who supported it went into business with the Soviets. Averell Harriman formed a joint shipping firm with the Soviets. The Rockefeller family became involved in the oil business with the Soviets. From the 1920s the Rockefeller's Chase Bank financed business in the Soviet Union. Today the Rockefeller's Chase Manhattan Bank maintains a branch office at 1 Karl Marx Square in Moscow.

As time passed, the list of American businessmen cooperating with the Soviets grew to include the heads of some of the largest corporations in the United States. For a more detailed study on this subject we recommend Antony C. Sutton's book *The Best Enemy Money Can Buy*, published by Liberty House Press, Billings, Montana.

To understand why wealthy businessmen in the United States have helped to establish and sustain what is commonly known as Communism, it is helpful to define some terms relative to the various economic systems of the 20th century.

Communism is defined by *The American Heritage Dictionary* as, "A social system characterized by the absence of classes and by common ownership of the means of production and subsistence." No nation existing during the 20th century fits this definition of Communism. There have been many communistic experiments (several in the U. S.) in which a community of people has voluntarily attempted to live together under such a system; however, none of these have ever been successful in improving the quality of life or remaining in existence for a long period.

Communism, as laid down by Karl Marx in *The Communist Manifesto*, was a call to establish Socialism. His ten point plan for the takeover of industrialized nations included: Abolition of private property, a graduated income tax, abolition of right of inheritance, government confiscation of property, a national banking system, communication and transportation under control of the state, instruments of production owned by the state, forced labor, population control, and free education in public schools. These are all socialist measures leading to total government. According to Marx, only after socialism had been established would the all powerful state melt away and Communism come into being. Needless to say, no all powerful state has ever voluntarily given up its military and police power.

The term "Socialism" is defined by *The American Heritage Dictionary* as, "A social system in which the producers possess both political power and the means of producing and distributing goods." This, of course, describes an economic dictatorship controlled by government.

The term "Capitalism" is also misused and misunderstood. Capital is defined by *The American Heritage Dictionary* as, "Any form of material wealth used or available for use in the production of more wealth." Some of the basic forms of capital are money, tools, and natural resources. All systems use money, tools, and natural resources. All are capitalistic.

The basic conflict concerning capitalism is not the use of capital, but who controls the capital. Socialism is a capitalistic system controlled by government. Competitive free-enterprise is a capitalistic system controlled by individuals, without government interference. Monopolistic capitalism is privately controlled but protected from competition by government.

With this understanding it is easier to see why wealthy American capitalists, who wish to avoid competition by owning government protected monopolies, support revolutionary leaders who are socialists. Monopolistic capitalism is only made possible by a partnership with, or control over government. Monopolies are impossible without government protection.

What is known as Communism has been characterized by forced collectivism on one hand and government protected monopolies on the other. Thus, while the Soviet Government was taking away the private property of its citizens and forcing them to work in collectives, such as farms, factories etc., it was also in partnership with, and protecting the business monopolies of wealthy American businessmen who helped to finance the revolution.

The system that benefits the greatest number of people is a competitive free-enterprise system. A good way to illustrate this is to explode the socialist myth that, under free-enterprise, employers exploit their workers.

On July 10, 1905, a speech was given at Union Temple Hall in Minneapolis by socialist Daniel De Leon. The speech "Socialist Reconstruction of Society" was later printed in the tens of millions of copies in principal languages around the world. According to Dr. Howard E. Kershner in his book *Dividing The Wealth: Are You*

Getting Your Share?[7] the essence of De Leon's speech was that, according to government statistics, labor's share of manufactured wealth was on the average 20 percent while the owner's share was 80 percent.

The tragedy of De Leon's conclusion was that it was just the opposite of the truth. As it turned out, De Leon made a colossal mistake because he only considered the cost of labor in the final stage of manufacturing, overlooking the cost of labor along the line from raw material to finished product. When all of the cost of labor is added up, labor gets the 80 percent, owners get the 20 percent. Out of the 20 percent must then come the expense of overhead, taxes, etc. until finally, the net profit is often as low as 2 or 3 percent, or, no profit at all.

Actually, according to U. S. Department of Commerce figures, the worker's share is 87.5 percent and the owners' share is 12.5 percent. Compare this with socialist nations around the world where workers receive barely enough of produced wealth to exist, the government getting the rest.

Having failed in their first attempt to get the United States to join the League of Nations, the War-makers set out to create a conflagration so terrible that the aftermath would sweep the entire world into a one world government.

The same powerful financial interests that worked to get the United States into World War I worked with the now well-established Council on Foreign Relations to set the stage on both sides of the ocean to create World War II.

The man they chose to promote as a leader in Germany was Adolf Hitler. The conditions that would enable them to bring Hitler to power had already been established by the signing of the Treaty of Versailles that placed impossible reparations demands upon the German government as a result of World War I. British Foreign Secretary, Lord Curzon, who was a delegate to the conference at Versailles stated that, "this is no peace; this is only a truce for twenty years."[8] In exactly 20 years (1939) the war began.

As a result of the treaty's demands for reparations, (269 billion marks) the German government resorted to inflation of the currency to comply. The resulting inflation (printing of unbacked currency) wiped out the middle class and brought economic collapse to the nation. The extent of this inflation was so great that a pound of butter that cost 3 German marks in 1918 cost six-trillion marks by 1923. Toward the end, 100 million marks would not even buy a box of matches. The crisis having been created, the solution was then offered, a man on a white horse to save the nation. Adolf Hitler was promoted as that man and eventually he and his Nazi party came to power in Germany.

Hitler had two main supporters, Wall Street in the United States, and the I. G. Farben company in Germany. The I. G. Farben company was a beneficiary of the Dawes Plan, which was initiated in the United

States after World War I and backed by the Council on Foreign Relations. This plan called for massive loans to Germany. Under this plan I. G. Farben received a loan of $30 million from the Rockefeller's National City Bank.

It would not have been possible for the German war machine to have been rebuilt after World War I without help from financial circles in the United States. The Krupp munitions works was salvaged by a $10 million loan from companies in New York, as was the Farben controlled steel works with a $100 million loan.

In 1928 John D. Rockefeller, Sr. formed a partnership with I. G. Farben creating interlocking business interests around the world. Throughout World War II this was kept secret by a complicated network of companies set up for that purpose.

American technology, engineering, and entire companies went to Germany. Many of these companies made profits supplying war materials for both sides of the war. While American companies were making profits on the German side, I. G. Farben was making profits on the American side.

During the Nuremberg Trials it was learned that the business leaders of I. G. Farben had controlled the Nazi state. Farben operated such concentration camps as Auschwitz and Buchenwald. Although Farben was the backbone of the Nazi war machine, its influence was so great that its headquarters buildings in Frankfort, Germany were off limits to American bombardiers. These buildings survived the war unharmed.

Today the interlocking Farben and Rockefeller interests are the largest chemical and drug cartel in the world. This cartel plays a major role in the promotion of drug-oriented medicine and against the use of natural products, such as vitamins, especially in controlling cancer.

For more information about the Farben, Rockefeller drug cartel, we recommend G. Edward Griffin's book *World Without Cancer: The Story of Vitamin B17*. It is available from American Media, P. O. box 4646, Westlake Village, California.

To accomplish their war-making plans on this side of the ocean, the international bankers set up a money crisis in the United States. The crisis was the Great Depression of 1929. The solution offered was to make a socialist nation out of the United States.

The first step was for the Federal Reserve to expand the money supply by 62 percent between 1923 and 1929, thus creating a false aura of prosperity. It was then made possible to purchase stocks on extensive credit with bank loans to cover up to 90 percent of the purchase. The catch was that these loans could be called in at any time, and if called in, had to be repaid within 24 hours.

To cover themselves, the Money Barons got out of the stock market before they started calling in the 24 hour loans. The panic that followed caused the market to crash resulting in bank runs that forced thousands of banks to close. While this was going on, the Federal Reserve did nothing to relieve the situation. To make matters worse, the Federal Reserve reduced the money supply by more than a third between 1929 and 1933, doing just the opposite of what it had supposedly been created to do.

Those in on the game sold their stock at the peak of the market, and bought it back for five cents on the dollar. Thus, they made vast fortunes out of the misfortunes of others. The Great Depression was actually a massive transfer of wealth, out of the hands of the American people who had worked to create it, and into the hands of the Money Barons who had engineered the stock market crash.

While the American people were being set up for financial disaster, the perpetrators were also working to get their man into the White House. The man they selected was a Harvard graduate whose family had been in New York banking since the eighteenth century. Their candidate had pursued a career on Wall Street and was on the board of directors of eleven corporations. He was first backed for governor of New York and then for president of the United States. To gain the confidence of the international socialists, he had written an article for the Council on Foreign Relations showing his support for world government. This article was published in their magazine, *Foreign Affairs,* in July 1928. It may have been more than coincidental that he also lived in a house next door to the Council on Foreign Relations' headquarters in New York.

Following the pattern of "promising the opposite of what you intend to do," this candidate was sold to the American people as "a man of the little people" who would stand up to Wall Street. And, so it was that in 1932, Franklin D. Roosevelt was elected president of the United States.

As soon as Roosevelt was installed in office, the movement to socialize the United States began. This revolutionary plan was known as the "New Deal." The main agency created to carry out the revolution was the National Recovery Act (NRA). It was headed by representatives from Wall Street and big business.

These socialists set out to regulate prices, wages, and working conditions throughout America. Controls were carried to such an extreme that a New Jersey tailor was fined and jailed for pressing a suit for five cents lower than the government allowed. Every move upon the part of the socialist planners served to prolong the depression, with unemployment being greater at the end of Roosevelt's first term in office than at the beginning.

One event that slowed, but never stopped, America's descent into socialism was the Supreme Court's labeling of the fascist (merging of state and business) measures of the National Recovery Act as unconstitutional.

Although slowed down in their plans to socialize the United States, the planners continued to work toward conditions that would lead to world government. While secretly preparing for war, Roosevelt, like Wilson, campaigned for reelection on a pledge that "Your boys are not going to be sent into any foreign wars."[9] When Tyler Kent, a code clerk at the American embassy in London, tried to reveal secret dispatches between Churchill and Roosevelt, and warn the American people of Roosevelt's intention of getting the United States into war, he was imprisoned in England until the war was over. By that time Roosevelt was dead.

The power behind Roosevelt getting the United States into World War II was the Council on Foreign Relations. Under a program financed by the Rockefeller Foundation, (the War and Peace Studies Project) the CFR conducted 362 meetings and prepared 682 papers for the President and the State Department. This CFR campaign was conducted in secret, and began just two weeks after Britain and France declared war on Germany.

In 1940, CFR members ran an appeal for United States entry into the war in newspapers across the country. Their plan was for a union of the United States and England into a permanent Atlantic alliance as a major step toward world government.

While America's secret government wanted war, the American people did not. In 1940, a Gallup poll found that 83 percent of Americans were against going to war in Europe.

Ignoring the desires of the American people, and without a declaration of war by Congress, Roosevelt began to provoke Germany and the Axis powers by aiding Britain with fifty destroyers and hundreds of millions of rounds of ammunition. All German consulates were closed, and U. S. ships were ordered to sail into war zones and, in some cases, to depth-charge German U-boats.

Japan was also provoked. The Secretary of War, Henry Stimson, (a CFR member) met with Roosevelt to discuss how to get Japan to make the first overt move to start a war with the United States. As a result, a trade embargo against Japan was enacted, Japan's assets in the U. S. were frozen, and the Panama Canal was closed to its ships. In addition, an ultimatum was sent to Japan setting conditions in order for trade to resume. Eleven days later the Japanese attacked Pearl Harbor leaving over two thousand Americans dead and eighteen naval vessels sunk or damaged. War in the Pacific had begun.

It is now well documented that Roosevelt and George Marshall knew ahead of time that the Japanese were going to attack, but kept this information from the commanders at Pearl Harbor. An authoritative book on this subject is John Toland's *Infamy: Pearl Harbor and Its Aftermath.*

And what was the aftermath of World War II that, like World War I, left millions of French, German, British, and American soldiers dead? The Soviet Union greatly expanded its territory, fortunes were made by international business cartels, and the world was moved closer to a one world government.

Presidents Roosevelt's closest advisor during the war was Harry Hopkins, a zealous admirer of the Bolsheviks.

After the war, two congressional hearings examined evidence that Hopkins had given the Soviets nuclear materials for making the atomic bomb. These shipments were revealed because of the records of lend-lease expediter, Major George Racy Jordan in his book *From Major Jordan's Diaries.* Under the lean-lease program $11 billion in aid was sent to the Soviet Union.

Chapter 11

Babylon's War Against God

And I saw the woman drunken with the blood of the
saints, and with the blood of the martyrs of Jesus: . . .
Revelation 17:6

And in her was found the blood of prophets, and of
saints, and of all that were slain upon the earth.
Revelation 18:24

The rise of a Modern Day Babylon during the 20th
century has had the distinction of making this the
bloodiest period in history. Above the lust for wealth and
power, upon the part of the leaders of this infamous
structure, has been a Satanic drive to carry out the
Illuminist plan to destroy all traditional religion and
replace God with the state, and an idolatrous worship of
nature.

This plan has been carried out in such a consistent,
long range, and universal manner that it is impossible not
to have been the policy of a central power. The victims
of this policy, those who believed in God as a creator,
have numbered in the tens of millions, most of whom
have been murdered by a government that Modern Day
Babylon brought to power.

Amazing as it is, and for whatever reason, these outrages have occurred without a cry of protest upon the part of many of the world's most well known religious leaders. Like the Priest and the Levite (in the story of the good Samaritan) who ignored the plight of the man who was beaten and robbed by thieves, they too have "passed by on the other side."

It is not well known that one of the first countries to become a victim of the war on religion during the 20th century, and the first country in this hemisphere to be betrayed into Communism, was Mexico. To realize the full import of this, it is necessary to review some of Mexico's history leading up to these events.

Before the 19th century, primarily through the efforts of the Catholic Church, the inhabitants of Mexico were elevated to a settled Christian people, unified by a common faith, and possessing the arts and industries of a self-sustaining civilization. This was no less than a miracle of transformation from hostile nomadic tribes, speaking different languages, and ruled by the Aztecs who annually sacrificed tens of thousands of human beings upon their polytheistic altars.

The University of Mexico was established in 1553, almost a hundred years before Harvard. From the sixteenth to eighteenth century, it produced a series of native poets, dramatists, historians, jurists, scientists, and journalists of such excellence that North America had little comparable. Mexico had the first printing press in the new world. It was engaged in printing catechisms, school texts, and Bibles. Evidence of culture was found in the churches that dotted the land, many of which had schools and hospitals in connection with their work.

Agriculture flourished and, by 1810, some exports were on a par with the United States. Many manufactured goods competed with England in volume. Everything about Mexico bore the fruits of a happy and industrious people led to this plateau of greatness by the love and leadership of the dedicated priests and nuns of the Catholic Church.

The decline of Mexico started when religious influence began declining after the king of Spain, Charles III, expelled the Jesuits in 1767 and the state seized the Jesuits' Pious Fund of some forty-five million dollars. This money had been used by the Jesuits to lend to small farmers at 5 percent interest, with the interest being used for charity.

When the Cadiz Constitution of 1820 restricted the rights and liberties of the Church, and The Cortes rejected Mexico's submitted Guarantees of Religious Independence and Union, Royalist leader Iturbide was proclaimed Emperor of an Independent Mexico.

But a peaceful and prosperous Mexico, united by a common religious faith, was not allowed to continue. The events that followed were replays of the events of the French Revolution, and like that revolution, began in the Illuminist Lodges. These lodges had been imported into Mexico by way of France, Spain, and the United States.

The first United States Minister to Mexico, Joel R. Poinsett (1825-1829), was involved in the spread of Illuminist lodges into Mexico. Together, these Illuminist controlled lodges built an occult political machine out of which came the "liberal" leaders that used the power of government to wage war on religion.

In 1827, a four-point program for this purpose was adopted in secret sessions in New Orleans by Poinsett and his pro-American liberal party. This platform eventually became law in Mexico and led to the absolute freedom of an anti-Christian press and speech, and absolute suppression of all others. It also led to the elimination of most of the monks and monasteries, Christian teachers and clergy, and the confiscation of all Christian schools, and institutions. As in the French Revolution, the battle cry was "liberty and equality."

According to Michael Kenny, the author of *No God Next Door,* the Juarez code (1858-1871) formed the basis of a constitution that legalized the destruction of the Church that followed in the 20th century. Kenny wrote that:

> The Juarez laws abolished all religious orders and confraternities, dress, vows, teachers, and teaching, with practically all civil rights and legal personality; nullified Christian marriages, and penalized religious rites and insignia anywhere outside the Church walls. Churches and all religious institutions were declared the property

of the State, which instituted a "National Church" of its own and invited United States sects to replace them; and "God" was eliminated from oaths and textbooks and civil formalities.[1]

When the Mexican people rose up against Juarez, and elected a new government, the United States broke off diplomatic relations with the new government and supported Juarez to the point of military action. This began a policy carried out by the United States government throughout the 20th century. The agents that have carried out such policies have all worked toward a common long-range goal, and have generally had ties to a center of power that we have described as "Modern Day Babylon."

By 1876, the accession of Porfirio Diaz to president tempered the States' war against the Church and by the end of the Diaz period the Church was conducting some 2,000 free schools and colleges, and a new network of hospitals and institutions. These were maintained by clergy and sisterhoods dependent entirely upon charity. This continued up to the presidency of Huerta when according to Kenny:

> . . . President Wilson supported with army and navy the worst scoundrels that ever raped and pillaged Mexico; whence issued the orgy of anarchy and tyranny that culminated in Calles.[2]

The scoundrels that president Wilson chose to support were eventually led by Plutareo Elias Calles. Although Calles, known as the Supreme Chief, was for a long time the dominate force in the atheistic socialism of Mexico, he was never able to produce his record of birth as a citizen of Mexico.

As a primary school teacher, and municipal treasurer at Guaymas, he was dismissed for immorality and disappearance of funds. He then rose from bartender to owner of the Elias hotel, which burned under conditions that prevented insurance from carrying the loss. In 1911 he was police chief of Agua Prieta, and owner of a saloon and gambling hall. He made this the only one in town by killing his rival and taking his goods. Patronage of brothels, and seizure of women, earned him some unprintable names.

Captured in 1912, he was saved from execution by Dr. Manuel Huerta whom he later hanged. In 1922 he violated United States territory by sending men to kidnap and murder General Blanco and Colonel Martinez who were refuges in Laredo, Texas. Officials in Laredo were prevented from taking legal action against Calles because of diplomatic immunity being conferred on him by the United States Secretary of State.

Rising with Obregon into prominence among the Carranza-Villa bandits of Sonora, Calles was rewarded with the governorship of Sonora and later the presidency of Mexico as successor to Obregon.

If it seems impossible that President Wilson could back such a man, it should be remembered that the influence behind Wilson throughout his career as president was Colonel Edward Mandel House, the Marxist (Communist) who founded the Council on Foreign Relations, and the man whom Wilson called his "alter ego."

It was under Calles that some of the most outrageous attacks on religion occurred. These attacks began with Calles taking away the right of the parents to educate their own children, and declaring his intentions to take possession of the consciences of the children and to create a new national soul. In a message to the nation from the Governors palace of Jalisco Calles stated:

> We must enter into consciences and take possession of them: the conscience of the children and the conscience of the youth; for the youth and the child must belong to the Revolution.[3]

This declaration was based on the belief that the child belongs to the state, and only the state has the right to educate the child, and that all religion must be excluded from his teaching. This was the same philosophy adopted by the leaders of the French Revolution, and unfortunately, it is the same philosophy held by leading educators in the United States.

Another prominent leader in the war against religion was Garrido Canabal, governor of Tabasco and a favorite of Calles. Canabal declared that education must be socialist and scientific, and that social relations which are based upon sex must be exemplified scientifically. To demonstrate the social relations, boys and girls were stripped naked in the government schools to see with their own eyes the facts of sex.

When government schools were boycotted, police and soldiers were sent out to seek the children and force them into the classrooms. At Naco, Sonora, children were beaten when they refused to repeat, "No hay Dios" (There is no God.) but cried out, "Hay Dios, hay Dios." At one point, the Secretary of State put out an order that children everywhere be gathered into Sunday services to decry God and religion and glorify atheism and socialism.

Free tickets were distributed to the lewdest movies and school children were taken to maternity hospitals to witness births. Classrooms were adorned with such pictures as a monk and nun in lustful approach eagerly disrobing. Music was also used to "defanaticize" the minds of the masses.

Anti-Christian fanaticism even extended to the graveyards where monuments with Christian names and symbols were removed and numbers only were allowed to be used to identify the dead. Public mockery resulted in the naming of a prize bull "God" and a donkey "Pope." In Guadalajara, fifteen year old boys and girls were stripped naked and forced to participate in mock baptisms.

Garrido Canabal, who under Calles planned and carried out such conscience killing devices, had been sent to Russia to study the Soviet education system.

Under Calles 90 percent of the churches, and all Catholic schools and convents were confiscated and closed. Only twenty-five priests were allowed to minister to the 1,700,000 people in the Federal District. Priests were banned from fourteen states, many being tortured and slain. All bishops were listed for expulsion and amendments were posted in Congress demanding their death.

Typical of Socialist regimes, every excuse was used to confiscate private property, even homes where church services were held, or priests were hidden. Rewards were offered to those who would report such "criminal offenses."

Through all of this, the blood of a gentle and devout people was being shed. The savagery against those who protested was such that on one occasion hundreds of women and children lay wounded or dying in the streets.

When 10,000 students and 60,000 parents marched in protest to Calles' educational program, the United States Ambassador, Josephus Daniels, came to his aid with American support and eulogies to "Mexico's strong man."

When the Mexican people rose up in arms against sacrilege, rape and rapine (the Cristero period 1926-1929) and Calles forces were in danger of being overthrown, American combat planes were sent to drop tons of gas bombs and incendiary grenades on the freedom fighters. The only things the United States government showed any interest in protecting were the antireligious dictators and American oil, mineral, and banking interests.

Efforts to take the story of the plight of Mexico to the American press were effectively blocked by a censorship of silence. When a famous international reporter went to Mexico and wrote an authentic account of the events taking place, no large North American newspaper would print it. The New York Daily wanted the story, but the millionaire owner forbid the editor to touch it. By this time (1928), the Money Barons in New York had purchased control of the major newspapers in the United States and Mr. McCullagh had to go to England to find a publisher.

Although the Socialist rulers of Mexico spent millions of dollars on propaganda in U. S. newspapers, the truth did eventually begin to filter through. Much of the credit for the circumventing of the censorship was due to the efforts of the Knights of Columbus. As a result, protests from across America began to flow into Congress, the Senate, and the State Department. This resulted in a resolution of Congress (the Borah Resolution) calling for a Congressional investigation into the matter. Resolutions were also passed by six state legislatures supporting the Borah Resolution. Protestant, Catholic, and Jewish leaders also supported it.

As could be expected, the U. S. State Department opposed any investigation into the Mexico-American scandal. The tragedy in Mexico, and other similar events supported by the State Department throughout the 20th century, indicate that the plans of the trustees of the Carnegie Endowment for International Peace to control United States foreign policy had indeed become a reality.

In the light of the circumstances, the ability of the people of Mexico to retain their Christian heritage is a tribute to their civilization. That they continue to come across the border into the United states by the millions is a sure sign that the socialist wreckers of their nation still control Mexico.

At the same time that the ground-work for a war against religion in Mexico was being laid, a war against religion was getting under way in the country that was to become the Union of Soviet Socialist Republics (U.S.S.R.). In many respects, the background of events leading up to, and during, the horror that occurred in the Soviet Union was similar to that which occurred in Mexico and France.

The seeds of revolution had been planted in Russia as early as the eighteenth century by Illuminated Free Masonry moving into Russia from Germany and France. The scholar Barruel (writing in 1798) had this to say about French involvement:

The Sect (the Illuminati) had many adepts in Russia whom it taught to scoff at oaths; and they only took the oath of fidelity to the monarchy, that they might the more easily annihilate the Russian diadem. The conspirators were headed by *Genet*, heretofore the agent for the cabinet of Versailles, but now become the agent of the Jacobins.[4]

The influence of the Illuminati reached to the Czarist Court of the Romanoffs due to the success of Weishaupt's followers in placing their members as tutors to the sons of the wealthy and powerful, especially to those who were likely to become rulers.

When the time finally came for the overthrow of the Czar in 1917, the man the powerful elite in the United States chose to support had a venomous hatred toward God. This is the way Lenin himself expressed his hatred:

Every religious idea, every idea of a god, even flirting with the idea of god is unutterable vileness of the most dangerous kind, disease of the most abominable kind. Millions of sins, filthy deeds, acts of violence and physical contagions are far less dangerous than the subtle, spiritual idea of a god decked out in the smartest "ideological" costumes.[5]

That war against God is the main driving policy of Communism was explained by Aleksandr Solzhenitsyn:

Within the philosophical system of Marx and Lenin, and at the heart of their psychology, hatred of God is the principal driving force, more fundamental than their political and economic pretensions. Militant atheism is not merely incidental or marginal to Communist policy; it is not a side effect, but the central pivot.[6]

To carry out this policy in the Soviet Union, tens of millions of innocent human beings were systematically tortured, and murdered. Out of 60,000 churches in 1914, by 1941 only 100 remained. While all of this was going on, it was business as usual for the American businessmen who helped set up the Soviets. For the majority of church leaders in America, it was silence.

As was the case with Mexico, when the Communist government was about to fall it was the United States government that came to its rescue. This crisis came about when Stalin's government was bankrupt and staying alive by check kiting. At this point President Roosevelt gave the Communists diplomatic recognition, making it possible for them to obtain credit. From that time on the United States government has done everything possible to help the Communist leaders in the Soviet Union stay in power.

Although ignored by the CFR-controlled American news media, much of what is known about past and present conditions in the Soviet Union has been revealed by defectors. One of these important defectors is Lev Alburt, a Soviet scientist who became an International Chess Grandmaster in order to escape and become an American citizen. Twice he earned the title "U. S. Chess

Champion." In a 1988 interview Mr. Alburt had this to say about religion in the Soviet Union:

There is no religious freedom in Soviet Russia today in the American sense of the word religious freedom. Immediately after the Revolution, Lenin destroyed the Russian Church and destroyed physically people who were servants of the church, priests, and officials who were servants of other religions. Also many people who just believed in God and who didn't want to switch to Atheism were physically destroyed.

I think it can be explained why Communist rulers in virtually all countries, in Russia, China, Cuba, have always been hostile to religion. A Communist regime is slavery, and the prime goal, the prime concern of Communist rulers is to convince their subjects that there is nothing in this world beyond materialist values, that there is no life after this life. And in order to have a good life, they should serve Communism well. And in this case they should, otherwise, they will be punished, and there are no other values for which you should receive rewards and take punishment.

Religious people believe in God, in a life hereafter, in certain religious and moral values. And a religious person when pressed too far by Communist authorities, is likely to say, 'I won't do it, I draw the line. I won't cross this line, no matter what you are going to do to me, or to my family. I won't do it because it is immoral. You can do to me whatever you want. I would rather die, but I won't commit this act of betrayal of morality.' And therefore, for Communist rulers, religion is a dangerous phenomenon. And they are doing everything they can to discredit, and destroy religion. . . . [7]

Mr. Alburt also had this to say about those who have kept the Communists in power:

> Starting from the early days of the Soviet Regime, it couldn't possibly have survived without Western, and especially American help. All experts who came from Soviet Russia from the early 20s have been saying, 'don't help our oppressors!'[8]

The destruction of religion made possible in the Soviet Union by help from the United States has also been repeated in the Soviet's satellite nations in Eastern Europe. A knowledgeable authority on this subject is former United States Ambassador to Romania, David Funderburk, who spent six years living in Eastern Europe. Here are some of his first hand observations:

> In Romania, when I served as United States Ambassador, also subsequent to that, I was able to observe and witness through intelligence information, and otherwise, the steady, weekly destruction of churches, Pentecostal, Baptist, Brethren, Lutheran, Calvinist, Catholic, and Orthodox; the jailing of anybody who spoke out religiously, or who took part actively in a religious practice, and the murder of some Baptist and Pentecostal pastors and Catholic priests. All of this was taking place under Ceausescu, who at the time was given most favored nation treaty status by the United States. In other words, he was considered a favorite of Washington and the State Department, while at the same time he was carrying out a massive destruction of churches and religious believers.

> We don't have a profreedom foreign policy, carried out by the United States State Department or the United States Government which really benefits those who want to overthrow Communism and bring about freedom. Our policy has been geared toward helping salvage, and helping to bail out the Communist regimes, which are corrupt, and which are economic disasters.[9]

Just as the CFR's control over the mass media was used to withhold the truth of what was going on in the Soviet Union and Eastern Europe, this control is now being used to deceive millions of uninformed people into believing that everything has now changed, that the leaders in the Soviet Union are no longer Communists, but are now Socialists. We are told that these former Communists, overnight, out of the goodness of their hearts, decided to embrace capitalism and allow religious freedom. Since they are now our friends, we should supply them with massive amounts of foreign aid and support the "good guys" who are working against the "bad guys" in that country.

According to Anitoliy Golitsyn, the highest level Soviet official ever to escape to the West, this turnabout by Communist leaders is a total fraud, planned far in advance to deceive the West. Details of this planned deception are given in Mr. Golitsyn's book *New Lies For Old.* His book is available from General Birch Services, P. O. Box 8040, Appleton, Wisconsin.

Golitsyn's view is also shared by Ambassador Funderburk:

Contrary to what most of the media in America is telling us on a day to day basis, most of the countries in Eastern Europe are still Stalinistic, with very strong armed, repressive regimes. So that while we are hearing in the West that the East Block has collapsed, the Cold War is over, the Iron Curtain is cracking, and democracy, reform, and liberalism are everywhere, this of course is not the case.

The norm of existence for people in the East Block is still one of day to day persecution, day to day hardship, in effect slavery under a Soviet dominated system. And even in the two places where there have been some changes, Hungary and Poland, the Communists control the secret police, the military, and the presidencies of those countries,. . . [10]

The one solution consistently offered by men like Anitoliy Golitsyn and Ambassador Funderburk to reverse these conditions, and allow these enslaved nations to free themselves, is for the West to end all aid to Communist Block nations.

Not only has the foreign policy of the United states (under control of the CFR) been geared to raising up and maintaining Communist leaders, it has also been aimed at destroying anticommunists who have been friendly to the United States, especially sincerely religious leaders such as the former Chinese leader Chiang Kai-shek. Chiang Kai-shek could be described as the George Washington of his country, their lives being similar. Both were military men, both fought a revolution, both were Christians, and each became the head of his country.

Early in his life Chiang became a disciple of Dr. Sun Yat-sen (a Chinese physician and a Christian) and worked with him in his attempts to overthrow the corrupt Manchu dynasty and unify China under a constitutional republic. After training at a Chinese military academy, and at Japan's Military Staff College, Chiang rose rapidly in his military career under Sun Yat-sen.

In 1923, Dr. Sun Yat-sen sent Chiang to study the Bolshevik system in the Soviet Union. Here Chiang received insight into the communist system that enabled him to prevent an early attempt by the Communists to take over the government of China. Because of his observations Chiang wrote, "I became more convinced than ever that Soviet political institutions were instruments of tyranny and terror. . . . "[11]

Chiang's Christian conversion came about as a result of his marriage to Soong Mayling, the daughter of a prominent Chinese Methodist minister and Bible publisher. After careful study of the Bible, as he had promised Madame Soong that he would undertake, Chiang became a profound Christian for the rest of his life, regularly searching the Scriptures for guides to ruling China.

In 1928, Chiang answered a call to become chairman of the Nationalist Party's Central Committee. From this elevated position he and Madame Chiang were to exercise tremendous influence upon their people throughout China. Realizing that China needed a moral regeneration, he and Madame Chiang began what they called "The New Life Movement." This movement encouraged the people to follow the time-honored virtues of courtesy, honesty, service to others, and self respect. An outstanding example of Chiang's magnanimous Christian character was revealed in a Radio Chungking message given when World War II ended in 1945:

> I am deeply moved when I think of the teaching of Jesus Christ that we should do unto others as we would have them do unto us and that we should love our enemies. . . . We have always said that the violent militarism of Japan is our enemy, not the people of Japan. Although the armed forces of the enemy have been defeated and must be made to observe strictly all the terms of surrender, yet we should not for a moment think of revenge or heap abuses upon the innocent people of Japan.[12]

Although Chiang Kai-shek was a proven and loyal ally to the United States throughout World War II, a systematic campaign was carried out under the Truman administration to betray Chiang and bring the Communists to power in China. The Soviet Union had been allowed to come into the war, just six days before Japan surrendered, and then take over Manchuria. The vast amounts of Japanese military hardware captured was given to Mao's communist guerrillas and Manchuria was used as a stronghold from which to conquer China.

State Department aid to the Communists was so blatant that United States Ambassador to China, Patrick

Hurley, sent several foreign service officers home because of their pro-Communist activities. When they were promoted over his head, Ambassador Hurley resigned in disgust. He later testified that:

> The record of General Stilwell in China is irrevocably coupled in history with the conspiracy to overthrow the Nationalist Government of China, and to set up in its place a Communist regime — and all this movement was part of, and cannot be separated from, the Communist cell or apparatus that existed at the time in the Government in Washington.[13]

President Truman sent his Secretary of State, George Marshall, to China to pressure Chiang to form a coalition government with Mao's Communists. Marshall even wanted to send U. S. officers to train Communist guerrillas. This plan was blocked by Congress. Marshall later placed an arms embargo on military aid to the Nationalists. Although Congress appropriated $125 million for military aid to Chiang, the Truman administration ran such interference that only a small portion of it ever reached Chiang and it proved to be too little and too late. Chiang wrote in his diary that Marshall, "continues to try to accommodate the Communists in every possible way and force us to make concessions. He doesn't seem to care whether China survives or perishes. This indeed is a most painful situation."[14]

While all of this was taking place, a massive propaganda campaign in the United States sought to deceive the American people into accepting a Communist takeover of China. An excellent source of information about events during this time is John T. Flynn's book *While You Slept: Our Tragedy In Asia and Who Made it.* It was published by the Devin-Adair Company in 1951 and reprinted by Western Islands in 1965.

John T. Flynn was a graduate of Georgetown University, and had pursued a wide and varied career as a newspaper man being managing editor of the New York Globe, and a columnist for the New Republic and the Scripts-Howard newspapers. The author of several books, and a radio commentator, John T. Flynn was known for his careful and responsible handling of facts.

One thing that greatly puzzled Flynn was the way some of America's greatest newspapers, magazines, radio networks, and even motion picture producers supported the Communist takeover of China and slandered Chiang Kai-shek. Although many writers supporting Mao's communist guerrillas were later identified as Communists, the owners of the major news and entertainment media were certainly not Communists. What writers like Flynn did not know was that these powerful and wealthy businessmen, operating out of New York, and working through the major tax-free foundations and organizations like the CFR, had obtained control of the opinion molding media in the United States.

This control was so effective that out of 29 books about China written between 1943 and 1944, 22 of these were procommunist. These procommunist books all received favorable reviews and sold twenty times as many copies as the few anticommunist books. Among some of the leading magazines supporting Mao's Communists were: The Saturday Evening Post, Collier's Atlantic Monthly, and Harpers Companion.

The combined weight of all the forces against Chiang Kai-shek was so great that to keep a free China alive he had to flee to the island of Taiwan with two million of his followers. The aftermath of the establishment of two Chinas then allowed the world to see the fruits of two trees, one good and one evil.

Under Mao, the Communists murdered tens of millions of Chinese, waged war on religion, and brought China down to the level of the grinding poverty that is always the result of Socialism.

Under Chiang Kai-shek, Taiwan became a modern miracle of progress with a per capita income far exceeding that on the Communist mainland. On Taiwan, the Chinese people could enjoy representative government, and freedom of religion and expression on a level never before reached by the Chinese.

On April 5, 1975, the day of a Chinese holiday when the Chinese honor the memory of their ancestors, Chiang Kai-shek left this world at 10 minutes to midnight. The man who had written in his will that, "I have at all times considered myself a disciple of Jesus Christ,"[15] went to see his Master. After a beautiful sunny day on April 5, at midnight, just minutes after Chiang's passing, a terrible storm of rain, thunder, and lightning raged over the island causing sleepy Chinese everywhere to rise from their beds and gaze upon the storm. Whether this was chance or providence, no one knows.

The tragedy of the China story is that the most populous nation on earth, a nation that could have been one of the world's greatest examples of Christian leadership, was betrayed by the one nation that the world would least suspect, the United States of America. As has been stated by others who have commented upon this horrible betrayal, "May God forgive us!"

Cuba is another example of a land where God was banned. It is also an example of yet another country betrayed into Communist slavery by American hands. It would have been impossible for a known Communist terrorist (Castro) and his band of 83 men, holed up in the Sierra Maestra Mountains, to take over Cuba without powerful outside help. Where this powerful help came from was related by former United States Ambassador to Cuba, Earl E. T. Smith in his book *The Fourth Floor: An Account of the Castro Communist Revolution*. Smith served as ambassador during the time of Castro's rise to power (1957-58) and had first hand knowledge of these events.

The Cuban leader that our State Department said "had to go" was Fulgencio Batista, whom they called a "corrupt dictator." It is strange that when tens of thousands of Cubans were being murdered and imprisoned by Castro, the State Department never found it in their vocabulary to call him a "corrupt dictator."

The fact was, that in 1957 under Batista, Cuba had the highest standard of living in Latin America, 1957 being Cuba's most prosperous year. Wages were high and the Cuban peso was at parity with the dollar. Even though he was not without some faults, Batista had built roads, schools, and hotels, and had attracted foreign investors. Castro put an end to this progress and made Cuba a giant prison camp.

The methods used to establish a Communist dictatorship in Cuba were a replay of the methods used before. First a propaganda campaign was carried out against Bastista, then military arms were supplied to the revolutionaries. This was followed by an arms embargo against the Cuban government, and constant State Department pressure against Batista.

The top men in the State Department at this time, who were members of the New York based Council on Foreign Relations were: Secretary of State John Foster Dulles, Under Secretary of State Christian Herter, and Deputy Under Secretary of State Robert Murphy. The leader of the CIA was CFR member Allen Dulles, and the man who occupied the White House was CFR member Dwight D. Eisenhower. The tragic results of their actions, and inactions, are now history.

One American who became an eye witness to Castro's tyranny was Anthony Bryant, once a black revolutionary, who while in a Cuban prison discovered the truth about Communism, and at the same time discovered God. Bryant made national headlines when, in 1969, he hijacked a passenger jetliner and diverted it from Miami to Havana. His objective was to obtain arms to be smuggled back to the United States to be used to initiate guerrilla warfare here. Once in Cuba, however, Bryant was arrested and charged with sedition against the Cuban Government. He was sentenced to 12 years in prison, not because he hijacked a jetliner or robbed the passengers on board, but because one of the men he robbed was a secret Cuban agent working in the United States. The agent had to go underground because of his exposure.

After spending 12 years in Cuban prisons, Bryant was among several prisoners allowed to return to the United States during a public relations campaign put on by Castro. Bryant then traveled all over the United States telling of his experience in Castro's Marxist Utopia. Here are some of his eyewitness accounts:

> First of all, I'll tell you that I expected to find a government which would be caring, kind, and really considerate of its population. However, I found that it was really the exact opposite. I witnessed beatings there, I think I probably witnessed thousands in the 12 years I was in Cuba. It was a situation where it was a daily

occurrence that the prisoners were beaten with machetes, which are long knives used to cut cane. I have been bathed in my own blood many times, and my skull has been fractured from machete blows from the guards.

I witnessed executions where they brought in the prisoners, and let thousands of people come in to witness it, and cheer the executioners on as they danced around their bodies.

I had a friend that they placed fish hooks through his eyelids, pulled them open, taped his eyelids open to his forehead, and kept a bright light beaming in his eyes all night while they beat him. Naturally he is blind today.

But I think basically the thing which impressed me, the most shocking to me, were the attacks that were made against the Christians, or those who believed in God, or wished to worship God. I witnessed the guards bringing in people whom they caught in the streets, in unauthorized services, let's say worshiping in a home, and they would bring them out on the patio, and beat them with machetes, and iron bars.

The first prison to which they took me had been a church which they had taken over. It had barbed wire around it, and the guards slept there. We the prisoners ate in the church on the first floor, and the warden had his office on the top floor. These were the things which really began to make me aware of the nature of the battle, or the struggle that we're involved in. It is indeed a battle between good and evil; between God and those who say that God is a lie, because that is exactly what the Communists state, that God is a lie, that he does not exist.[15]

In 1977, Nicaragua was a model for Latin American countries with freedom of the press, freedom of religion, private ownership of property, a free market economy, and open borders. Of all the Latin American countries, Nicaragua was among the top in human rights and living standards. Its political system was fashioned after the United States with a constitution and an electoral system based on two parties. Anyone over the age of 18 could vote.

The President of Nicaragua, Anastasio Somoza, was an admirer of the American form of government. From the age of 10, he had been educated in the United States and was a graduate of West Point. Somoza was a democratically-elected president with his main support coming from the poorer class that made up the bulk of the population. Much of this support was a result of the agricultural program that Somoza had put into effect that made it possible for the poor campesinos to acquire their own land.

Although Nicaragua had been the target of attacks by Communist Sandinista guerrillas, financed, trained, and armed by the Soviet Union and Cuba, those attacks were successfully repelled by the Guardia Nacional. Most of the Guardia Nacional officers had been trained in the United States.

The events that were to change Nicaragua from a free country to a slave state began one week after the inauguration of James Earl Carter as President of the United States in January 1977. From that point on, as expressed by former U. S. Ambassador to Cuba, Earl T. Smith, Nicaragua was to be "Cuba all over again."

High officials in the State Department who went along with Carter's destruction of Nicaragua were: Secretary of State and CFR member Cyrus Vance, Deputy Secretary of State and CFR member Warren Christopher, Assistant Secretary of State for Human Rights and CFR member Patricia Derian, and Ambassador to Nicaragua Lawrence Pezzulo also a member of the CFR. Jimmy Carter also became a CFR member after he left the White House.

Ignoring the murder of millions by the Communists, Communists that the CFR had put into power, the battle cry against Somoza was "human rights." A greater example of hypocrisy would be hard to find in the annals of history.

The scenario against Somoza was played out as usual, beginning with a massive smear campaign by the CFR-controlled media in the United States to condition the American people to accept a Communist take over of Nicaragua. Three American journalists whose perversions of truth did the most to help bring about the tragedy in Nicaragua were CFR member Dan Rather of CBS, CFR member Karen De Young of the *Washington Post*, and Alan Riding of the *New York Times*.

Before he was murdered, President Somoza was able to relate the results of an interview with Dan Rather that was aired in the United States on "Sixty Minutes":

> Rather tried every conceivable journalistic trick to trip me up on questions. He knew in advance the

answers he wanted and come "hell or high water" he was going to find the question to fit his preconceived answer. Well, he never succeeded. From watching the show, one would never know that Dan Rather spent two and one-half hours grilling me. It's difficult to believe, but Rather condensed that entire time to seven minutes. The remainder of the air time was devoted to old footage or other filming which he did in Nicaragua.

I didn't realize what the power of film editing really meant. With that power, Rather cast me in any role he chose. Every good thing I said about Nicaragua was deleted. Any reference to Carter's effort to destroy the government of Nicaragua was deleted. Every reference to the Communist activity and Cuba's participation was deleted.[16]

Media attacks were followed by an arms embargo against the government of Somoza and United States support of the Sandinista Communist leader Daniel Ortega.

As soon as the Communist Sandinista regime under Ortega took control of the government, the 8,000 member Guardia Nacional was imprisoned, private property confiscated, farms collectivized, and the media, schools, and churches turned into instruments of Communist indoctrination. While this was going on, Jimmy Carter was sending millions of dollars to the illegal Communist government under Ortega.

The Communist takeover of Nicaragua culminated in a war against religion that resulted in horrible atrocities against the Christian Miskito Indians when they refused to accept Marxist propaganda.

One American who witnessed the results of these atrocities was David Courson, a former U. S. Marine and Vietnam combat veteran. As head of an organization known as Christian Emergency Relief Team (CERT), Courson and his volunteer medical teams made dozens of trips to the remote border areas of Nicaragua and Honduras to aid refuges from Communist Nicaragua. This is the story of the Miskito Indians as related by David Courson:

> In the 1840s and 1850s, missionaries from the Moravian Church in Germany, Protestant Evangelical Missionaries, brought the Gospel to the Miskito, the Suma, and the Rama Indians who are direct descendants of the Mia Indians.
>
> These proud people, these industrious people, lived in relative obscurity as hunters, as fishermen, as farmers, throughout the 1800s and on through 1979, when the revolution took place inside Nicaragua with outside Communist influence ousting Mr. Somoza. As a result, the Soviet Union moved in quickly, propped up Daniel Ortega, and other Sandinista leaders, which subsequently led to the persecution of the church inside Nicaragua.
>
> Persecution has included the burning of the Bibles in the villages. The Sandinista government sees the Bible as contrary to liberation theology and Marxist-Leninist teaching inside Nicaragua. Pastors have been killed, entire villages have been wiped out. In 1981, the decision was made simply to eliminate 60,000 people from the

face of the earth along this area because of their refusal to adopt and to embrace Marxist-Leninist philosophy.

An example of the extent of the persecution can be illustrated by a 25 year old pastor by the name of Biardo, who was awakened early one morning when Sandinista troops came into his village. They called all of the men together outside the church, gave them shovels, had them dig their own graves, and shot them in the back. The women and children were taken inside the church, and there in front of Pastor Biardo they were violated and tortured in such ways that I cannot begin to describe to you today.

The pastor was mocked, tied up to a pole, spat upon, and the Sandinista troops said, "Where is your God? Why doesn't He ever hear you? Why doesn't He ever answer your prayers?" They set the church on fire. The pastor was soon terribly burned on his arms, legs, his hands and feet; and a result of the fire was that the ropes that bound him were also burned through. He was then able to rescue some of the people inside the church. They made their way through the jungle, hiding in the daytime, and traveling at night, in what has come to be known as The Trail of Tears, to one of the refugee camps along the Honduras Nicaragua border inside Honduras. That is but one example of the persecution of the church in Nicaragua.[17]

The story of Africa is another story of the betrayal of an entire continent into the hands of those who hate Christianity. Out of 52 nations, the vast majority are ruled by one-party dictatorships with no chance for democratic reforms. The truth about these betrayals, and the resulting war against religion, has been withheld by the news media, and ignored by the major religious denominations in America. Whenever the U. S. news media covered events in Africa, the news has always been slanted toward Communist goals and against freedom, South Africa being the greatest victim of this bias.

Missionary director Peter Hammond, a native of South Africa, related this about the moral conditions in his country:

> You hear so much bad news about South Africa, none of which really bears any resemblance to the reality in South Africa. One thing people would be surprised to learn is what a moral and Christian country South Africa really is.
>
> For example, abortion is illegal in South Africa. You may not murder your unborn infants in our country. In addition to that, prayer, hymn singing, and Bible reading are a compulsory part of everyday school. Hymns are sung in the school, Bible reading and prayer at the beginning of each school and assembly, and we have religious instruction in classes. Pornography is banned in South Africa. For example, *The Last Temptation of Christ* was banned in our country. We also have compulsory church services in the military.
>
> Seventy-five percent of the population of South Africa attends church every week. But aside from that, we have a very high percentage of missionary minded, Bible believing, God fearing people who are very zealous for their faith.
>
> For example, South Africa is the largest Bible producing country in the world. America produces more

Christian books, and Christian tapes, than all the other countries put together, but South Africa produces more Bibles in more languages than any other country in the world.[19]

Peter Hammond also relates his eyewitness account of the Communist war against Christians in Africa:

When I was first called up to do my military duty in the South African Defense Force, back in 1979, we came across atrocities in South West Africa and Angola. SWAPO, the South West African Peoples Organization, the terrorist group backed by the Soviets, and funded by the World Council of Churches, has been involved in war to try and overthrow Mozambique for the last 20 years. In that time they've killed 10,000 civilians, largely through land mines.

We, as soldiers, had to sift through the wreckage of vehicles blown up by land mines, and we had to put the bodies into body bags. We had to sift through villages burned to the ground, and take the charred remains, the corpses of the people, and put them in body bags.

When we were involved in operations in Angola, we used to seek out the churches in the villages. We would go into a village and say, "Where is the church?" and every time the people would point to a burnt out place and say, "That was the church. The Cubans burnt it down." We would say, "Where is the pastor?" and the people would say, "The Communists shot him.' We would say, "What can we do to help you?" and the people would say, "Biblia, Biblia, — Bibles." Starving, hungry, thin people asked for Bibles as their first priority.

We've spoken to survivors during our missionary work during the last seven and one-half years in Mozambique and Angola. We have spoken to survivors of massacres, where Cuban troops walked into churches, took the Bible off the pulpit, threw it out the door, and said, 'OK, it's all over, just form a line, walk past the Bible, spit on the Bible and you can go free. If you do not spit, though, we will certainly kill you." And Christians in Angola had to make a choice sometimes, under the AK 47s of Cuban troops, whether to spit or die.[20]

The man backed by U. S. leaders to take over the government of South Africa is Nelson Mandela, a Communist terrorist and head of the African National Congress (ANC), a Communist dominated terrorist organization.

That Mandela was a Communist was proven when he was arrested and tried for treason by the South African Government. During the trial, articles and documents in Mandela's own handwriting were submitted to the court. In an 18-page document Mandela stated, "The people of South Africa, led by the South African Communist Party will destroy capitalist society and build in its place socialism."[21] In another document, entitled "Political Economy," Mandela wrote, "We communist party members are the most advanced revolutionaries in modern history. . . ."[22]

Although many blacks held elected positions in South Africa, until the national elections in 1994, Mandela was never elected to any government position by his people.

His power was acquired by the terror tactics of the ANC. One of the methods used by the ANC was known as "necklacing," whereby a victim was executed by first tying his hands and then placing an automobile or truck tire around his or her body, filling it with gasoline or diesel fuel, and setting it on fire. Most of the victims were not whites but blacks who refused to support the ANC. Winnie Mandela, the wife of Nelson Mandela stated, "With our boxes of matches and our necklaces, we shall liberate this country."[22] Hundreds of blacks have died an agonizing death by this method.

None of this deterred the United Nations, the U. S. Government, the World Council of Churches, the world news media, and many U. S. Congressmen and Senators from working for a new South African Government headed by the ANC. Under the CFR-dominated Carter administration, a U. S. boycott was launched against South Africa that helped set the stage for a Communist take over.

While the U. S. media was daily attacking South Africa, not a word was spoken about the millions of Africans who were dying because of Communist devastation in other nations throughout Africa. As hundreds of thousands of black Africans were fleeing from these Communist countries and pouring into South Africa to survive, the media attacks on South Africa continued.

It is a sad commentary indeed, that a once great nation has fallen so low, that Communist terrorists are given parades through the streets of New York, welcomed to the White House, and made heroes by America's news media.

Babylon's world wide wars against religion have not been limited to Christians and Jews, but have also extended to Muslims. The Soviet invasion of Afghanistan in 1979 was not the beginning of a world wide war against Islam, it was however, a major step in that direction.

Before the invasion, Afghanistan was a peaceful nation of 18 million people, 99 percent of whom were of the Islamic belief. The land area, about the size of Texas, is mostly mountains and desert. The climate is severe, very hot in the summer and very cold in winter. Although rich in minerals, the work force was 75 percent agricultural and 25 percent industrial with very little heavy industry.

The Soviet war against Afghanistan left more than 50 percent of its population killed, dispersed, or dead from disease or famine. Thousands of children were kidnaped and shipped to the Soviet Union for Communist training. The culture of the Afghan people, once known the world over for their jewelry and carpets, was almost totally destroyed.

The former economic advisor to the president of Afghanistan, Abdul Shams, recorded the full story of this horror in his book *In Cold Blood: The Communist Conquest of Afghanistan*. Following is the story that

Shams related on a radio broadcast in the United States. The story is given as it was expressed in Shams' words:

We saw their action in Afghanistan, what they mean when they talk of peace, when they talk of brotherhood, when they talk of friendship, what they mean when the Soviets took over Afghanistan militarily. On the first night they killed 17,200 people in the streets of Kabul. They have bayoneted pregnant women in Afghanistan. The children they have just torn apart. Even the unborn children which the ladies were bearing, they bayoneted their bellies and they took out unborn children and hung them up in the trees.

There was a special kind of torture they called West Torture. They hung them (captured freedom fighters) to two trees. They brought the trees down. They tied one hand to one tree and the other hand to the other tree. Then they left the trees back and they were torn apart.

In the countryside where the people are very devoted . . . The Soviets forcefully asked them to join the Communist party, to join them and to accept their alien policy and system. They refused, they said, "No, let us alone. We are Muslims and we are farmers. We are not politicians. Leave us alone."

But the Soviets were not satisfied . . . They went and destroyed their villages when they saw the resistance of the people. Some of the villages have been destroyed like there was no sign of life at all. They have destroyed almost 14,000 villages in Afghanistan. They have bombed, they have rocketed, they have burned.

Besides this the Soviets have dropped tiny anti-personnel bombs. These bombs were very sophisticated, made especially for children. They were very attractive to children. When a child picked these objects up—it was like tiny trucks, tiny cars, watches, pens, sometimes chewing gum, when they touched them or got them in their hands, their hands were blown off, their feet were blown off, their faces were torn off.[23]

And what of the attitude of American leaders toward Mikhail Gorbachev who was in power at the time Afghan children were being blown up? As soon as he was no longer the head of the Soviet Union he was welcomed to the United states where he is now free to travel, sell his books, and raise funds for his Moscow-based Foundation for Social, Economic, and Political Research. The U. S. Government even provides him with office space at the former Presidio Army Base in San Francisco. He is also aided in his fund-raising by a group financed by the Rockefeller, Carnegie, Mellon, Ford and other foundations. He was engaged by Senator Phil Gramm's Republican Senatorial Committee to speak at a Washington fund-raising event for which he was to receive $70,000.

But that's not all of the tragic story. The Soviet tanks that rolled into Kabul (the capital of Afghanistan) in 1979 were made in the Soviet Kama River Truck Plant. This plant (the largest in the world) was built by American businessmen and largely financed by American banks. The design, engineering, and key equipment all came from the United States. U. S. Government policy that made possible the American building of the Kama River plant involved CFR member Henry Kissinger, CFR member George Shultz, and CFR member Richard Nixon who was president at the time.

Even the highway that enabled Soviet tanks to reach Afghanistan was built by Soviet and U. S. engineers working side by side with U. S. foreign aid money footing part of the bill.

Although U. S. Government officials mouthed support for the Afghan freedom fighters, the end result was a sellout to a Soviet puppet government in Kabul.

The sellout in Afghanistan was not the end of war against Islam. The war did not end, the banners only changed from the Soviet flag to the United Nations flag. With the UN in the act, the war became world wide. The stage was set with the United States arming and supporting Muslim terrorist groups in Iran, Iraq, Syria, Libya, Algeria and a host of others. Although these terrorists groups are a tiny minority of the 800 million Muslims in the world, incidents created by them and highly publicized by the media can be used as an excuse to wage war against the innocent. The real criminals usually go unharmed.

The Gulf War is an example, among many that could be cited, of this kind of foul hypocrisy. This was the first time America initiated an unprovoked attack on a foreign power in another hemisphere. Prior to the war, the United States had engaged in a decade long build up of Saddam's war machine. In *The New American* magazine (March 21, 1994) William Jasper reported that:

> Investigations by the House Banking Committee and journalists have carefully documented a sordid trail of treachery and treasonous actions by George Bush and his retinue before, during, and after the Persian Gulf War.
>
> The U. S. provided or assisted Iraq in obtaining cluster bombs, technology for nuclear enrichment, U. S. designed munitions, missile technology, some $5 billion in loan guarantees, and much more.[24]

As is now well known, the major part of destruction during the Gulf War was upon civilian installations in Iraq resulting in the death of over 100,000 people, many of them innocent women and children. Saddam was unharmed. This was repeated in Somalia where the stated purpose of a UN invasion became the removal of General Mohammed Aidid, a Muslim leader who had been armed by the U. S. The UN occupation resulted in the killing and torture of Somali civilians, but not the capture of Aidid.

By March 1994, the UN war against Muslims had already resulted in 400,000 deaths in Iraq, Bosnia, and Somalia. These are called "peace" operations by the CFR-controlled news media. UN military forces are now in various stages of occupying at least ten Muslim countries with plans to occupy 19 more areas, many of which are Muslim. It is understandable that the United States is blamed for the actions of the UN since U. S. taxpayers furnish 30 percent of the UN operating budget, and 50 percent of the UN war budget.

There are several aspects of this CFR supported United Nations war against Muslims that Christians in America need to know. One is that the vast majority of true Muslims are peaceful, God-fearing people. The 800 million Muslims in the world stand in the way of a godless one world government, as do millions of Christians. Babylon's plan may be to promote warfare between the two by secretly promoting terrorism and placing the blame on the majority.

Another serious consideration for Christians in America is the increasing number of media attacks against "fundamentalism" under which are lumped groups like Operation Rescue, Zionists, and Muslims. If not stopped, UN troops may be used to wage war in the U. S. against Christians and Muslims, both being labeled as "Fundamentalists."

The tragic events at Waco may have been a test run to see if Americans have been sufficiently conditioned to accept military attacks by the government upon religion. As a warning to what may be planned, consider statements made by President Clinton (a member of the CFR) immediately after Waco:

> I hope very much that others who will be tempted to join cults and become involved with people like Koresh will be deterred by the horrible scenes they have seen.
> There is, unfortunately, a rise in this sort of fanaticism all over the world. And we may have to confront it again.[25]

Chapter 12

U. N. Modern Tower of Babel

> And the Lord said, Behold, the people is one, and they have all one language; and this they begin to do: and now nothing will be restrained from them, which they have imagined to do.
>
> Genesis 11:6

The potential for evil in the attempt to build the Tower of Babel, as recorded in the eleventh chapter of Genesis, was not in any threat to physically "reach unto heaven," nor was it in the desire to establish a city. The danger was in a concentration of power and the elimination of the division of nations established by Divine Providence.

A division of nations is of paramount importance because it has served to control the spread of evil throughout the earth. This is substantiated by Bible history in that the concept of nations was not established until after the universal flood of Noah's time. Prior to the flood, mankind had become so corrupted that, except Noah and those with him, all human inhabitants were destroyed. Immediately after the flood the concept of nations began, as recorded in Genesis chapter ten. From that time on, nations served as a check on each other throughout Old Testament history.

When the nations that occupied ancient Palestine became corrupted beyond redemption, the Israelites were sent to overcome them. This is made plain in Deuteronomy 9:5:

> Not for thy righteousness, or for the uprightness of thine heart, dost thou go to possess their land: but for the wickedness of these nations the Lord thy God doth drive them out before thee, . . .

Centuries later, when the Israelites had been corrupted to the point that they were burning their children to death as human sacrifices to Moleck, the ten northern tribes were invaded and deported by Assyria. To this day, these ten dispersed tribes have never been found.

The first attempt to circumvent the Divine order of sovereign and independent nations was frustrated by a division of languages, as recorded in Genesis 11:7, "Go to, let us go down, and there confound their language, that they may not understand one another's speech." This time those who wish to replace sovereign nations with a one world government have assembled with their interpreters. This time they have built a tower on the East River in New York. This time they plan to drive the concept of loyalty to God, family, and country off the earth.

The foundation for this modern Tower of Babel was laid at the founding conference of the United Nations in San Francisco in 1945. The man who was Secretary

General of the conference, and who helped draft the UN Charter, was CFR member Alger Hiss. Later, Hiss was discovered to be a Soviet spy and served time in prison for lying about his connections to a Soviet spy ring. In addition to Hiss, more than forty other American delegates to the UN founding conference were members of the CFR.

Alger Hiss took the UN Charter back to Washington in a small safe, and the U. S. Senate ratified the document without studying its contents. After the U. S. became a part of world government, John D. Rockefeller donated $8.5 million to purchase land for the UN building.

From the very beginning the UN was a big business proposition. Part of it was launched with the formation (by CFR members) of the International Monetary Fund (IMF) and the World Bank at the Bretton Woods Conference of 1944. Closely linked with Rockefeller's Chase Manhattan Bank, the World Bank has been used to lend money around the world, mostly U. S. taxpayers' money.

The beneficiaries of this money have not been the poor people in undeveloped countries, but wealthy industrialists who wish to expand operations in these countries. Congressman John Rarick explained it this way, "Aid to the poor countries usually ends up as seed money or loans to the wealthy industrialists from the developed countries to further their overseas operations in competition with the people whose country they claim to represent."[1] Since the end of WW II these loans, guaranteed by U. S. taxpayers, have served to expand the operations of international cartels and to advance their march toward a New World Order.

The major changes in the world throughout the 20th century have not occurred just because of an ideological conflict between Communism and Capitalism. Many of these changes have involved control of natural resources and markets by these cartels, many of whom are among the Fortune 500 businesses in America.

As mentioned in chapter 10, ever since the 1917 Revolution, American businessmen have operated government protected monopolies in the Soviet Union, with any form of private enterprise forbidden to any would be Russian entrepreneurs.

For example, Armand Hammer operated an asbestos mining and pencil manufacturing concession in the Soviet Union before and after WW II. While the Soviets were murdering millions of their own people, and turning the Soviet Union into a giant slave camp, Armand Hammer was making a profit. Hammer even worked out a grain deal so that he could ship grain to feed his mine workers. This was passed off as a humanitarian gesture to feed starving Russians.

Besides his business enterprises, Armand Hammer represented thirty-eight other American companies in the Soviet Union. This information is related in Carl Blumy's book *The Dark Side of Power*. Blumy was Armand

Hammer's public relations consultant for twenty-five years from 1955 to 1980.

Soviet defector Tomas Schuman related his interesting personal observations of relations between Communist leaders and American businessmen while he was assigned as a KGB operative in Moscow:

> I saw quite a number of influential Americans coming to Moscow. At that time I was working as a Junior Operative of my Novesti Press Agency which is a KGB controlled front. And very often when I met my foreign delegations in Moscow Airport, I saw private jet planes landing in a separate individual strip. Nice, well-dressed Americans would walk out and warmly embrace members of the Politburo. Kiss them, smooch them, like as if they were brothers, and great friends.
>
> When I asked my senior colleagues who they were, they would tell me, "Well, they are industrialists, and bankers, and members of elite groups." It didn't make much sense in my mind. They are supposed to be our enemies, the super capitalists of the United States. And when I kept on asking these dumb questions, naturally, my KGB supervisors told me to, "Shut-up and mind your own business," which I did of course.[2]

As to the attitude of the Russian people toward this business relationship between American businessmen and the Communists, Tomas Schuman had this to say:

> Most of the thinking people in my country hope that Americans will come to their senses and stop United States Government, multinationals, and superstructures

from aiding Communism. Giving money, credits, technology, spare parts, grain, and political recognition to a bunch of murders of my nation, who are quilty of killing sixty-six million of my population.[3]

For decades, the vast and rich mineral resources of the Soviet Union were kept locked up, except to the few. Then, suddenly, the Communist leaders had a change of heart, and the Iron Curtain came down. Outside of a few harmless shows to fool the West, this change occurred without internal revolt or bloodshed. Over-night the label was changed from Communist to Socialist, with the same leaders maintaining power under the new label. In reality, there had been no change in ideology at all since these leaders had always been socialists.

From that point forward, the rush was on for American companies to go into the Soviet Union, and many of its satellites, and, with loans backed by the U. S. taxpayers, open business partnerships with socialist governments. Nothing had changed except the expansion of a program that had been going on for decades.

Communist China is another example of such a business expansion with large American companies falling over each other to sign business contracts with the government. One of the reasons the slaughter of thousands of Chinese in Tiananmen Square was ignored by the United States was because three-hundred firms with annual sales of $7.5 billion wanted to do business as usual.

Why communist leaders cooperate in this is explained by Steven Mosher who was the first American student to live in China since it was taken over by the Communists:

The Chinese Communist party represents itself as the party of the masses, the party of the people. In fact, it's a very tiny elite which has greatly benefited from the dictatorship it has imposed on the Chinese people. The idea that Chinese Party rule will one day lead to a socialist utopia is nonsense. The only thing that Communist Party rule has done in the last forty years is that it has caused economic stagnation on the one hand, and terrible human suffering on the other.

The idea that there was somehow a tradeoff between bread and freedom, that if you lived in a poor country that people might choose Communism because it provided bread even if it didn't provide freedom of speech, and other forms of freedom of expression, is nonsense. We now know, especially in China, that the Chinese Communist party has provided neither bread nor freedom. They have provided nothing.

And the other thing one has to think about when one talks about hypocrisy in the Chinese Communist Party is, although they have a slogan of serving the people, in fact, Communist Party officials serve only themselves. And they have, over the last ten years, greatly benefited from the economic reforms.

They have taken payoffs from foreign companies, they take bribes from their own subordinates for promotion, and they take this money and invest it overseas. Now some of this money ends up in Swiss bank accounts, but a lot of it comes to the United states where it is invested in stocks and bonds, and real estate.

It turns out that nearly all of China's Communist Party elite have family members in the United States who come here to study in American universities, but have actually been sent here by their fathers to manage the family investments. For example Yang Shangkun the president, has a son in the United States. Li peng has a daughter in this country. And you cannot name a high ranking member of the Politburo or the Central Committee in China without finding that they have at least one family member in the United States to manage the family investments.[4]

After living and working in China for part of 1979 and 1980, Steven Mosher returned to the United States and wrote his nationally acclaimed book *Broken Earth: The Rural Chinese.* His shocking revelations about conditions in Communist China earned him the condemnation of the Beijing Government and denial of the doctorate degree in anthropology that he had earned at Stanford University.

China is but one example of changes in the world structure of nations since the end of WW II. At that time there were about fifty recognized nations. Now, near the end of the 20th century, they number over 180. Almost all of the newly established nations are in the socialist camp. All major changes have led the world closer to world government and the elimination of sovereign nations.

For anyone who wishes to learn more of the truth about United States involvement in changing the world during the 20th century, we recommend James Perloff's book *The Shadows of Power: The Council on Foreign Relations And The American Decline*. It is available from Western Islands, P. O. Box 8040, Appleton, Wisconsin.

Having established socialism throughout most of the world, the powerful internationalists working for world government then began planning to consolidate their power by way of a one world military force. A major step toward creating this world army began in 1961 with the publication of an official government document entitled *Freedom From War: The United States Program For General And Complete Disarmament In A Peaceful World*. This document, also known as Department of State Publication 7277, sets forth a series of measures that would totally disarm all nations, including the U. S., and place all weapons in the hands of the UN.

The War-makers who created the UN, and have been using war as a means to an end (world government), are now reaching for the ultimate power, a world-wide monopoly over military force.

Every U. S. president since 1961 has worked to carry out the treasonous steps of Department of State Publication 7277. Every military action upon the part of the United States since the end of WW II has served to erode United States sovereignty and to increase the military power of the UN. This includes Korea, Vietnam, the Gulf War, and Somalia.

Will the reality of an all powerful UN Army mean "peace" for the world? All recorded human experience of past ages answers with a resounding, "No!" In his well documented book *Global Tyranny . . . Step By Step: The United Nations and the Emerging New World Order* William F. Jasper refers to a study done by Professor R. J. Rummel about the human cost of 20th century totalitarianism. Dr. Rummel's investigation proved that, during the 20th century, and independent of war, all powerful governments have murdered over 119,000,000 of their own people. By comparison, the number killed on the battle field numbered approximately 35,000,000. This means that the total killed by governments in cold blood was almost four times that of war. William Jasper quotes Dr. Rummel as stating:

> Absolutist governments . . . are not only many times deadlier than war, but are themselves the major factor causing war and other forms of violent conflict. They are a major cause of militarism. Indeed, absolutism, not war, is mankind's deadliest scourge of all.[5]

The United Nations is not about "Peace and World Brotherhood." It is about war. If the War-makers are able to obtain a monopoly over military power, then, "nothing will be restrained from them, which they have imagined to do." This danger to mankind was one of the reasons that the builders of the Tower of Babel were stopped in chapter eleven of Genesis.

It is certain that a New World Order under the United Nations would mean the suppression of our God given rights protected by the U. S. Constitution, and the murder of millions of Americans by a Communist style dictatorship.

Having deceived much of the world, especially the American people, into believing that Communism is dead and that we can now live in peace and brotherhood, the Master Conspiracy behind the New World Order is now moving rapidly toward establishing an overt world dictatorship by way of an all powerful United Nations.

Because of numerous acts of treason upon the part of our leaders, the United Nations is now able to wage war around the world. These wars, in the name of peace, have already resulted in the killing of hundreds of thousands of innocent human beings. The greatest support for these wars has come from the United States, resulting in America rapidly becoming the most hated nation in the world.

It was never the intention of our Founding Fathers that we interfere in the affairs of other nations. George Washington especially warned against this. There is no place in the Constitution that gives anyone but Congress the authority to declare war against any nation. There is certainly no legal authority for a group of power-mad megalomaniacs to make the U. S. an international aggressor in order to create a New World Order.

The Master Conspiracy behind the New World Order is also using a more subtle means to conquer the world. This method is what some have referred to as the "treaty trap." It is just as deadly as war. It employs the age-old revolutionary scheme of creating a crisis and then offering a solution. The supposed crisis is man's destruction of the environment. The proposed solution is total control of the planet by the United Nations.

A giant step in this direction began in June of 1992, when between 20,000 to 30,000 participants from 178 nations attended the United Nations Conference on Environment and Development (UNCED) in Rio de Janeiro, Brazil. The overall goal of the conference was to "Save the Planet."

By what means they intend to do this was pointed out by the late Dixy Lee Ray, former member of the Atomic Energy Commission, assistant secretary of state in the U. S. Bureau of Oceans, and long-time member of the zoology faculty at the University of Washington. In her book *Environmental Overkill: Whatever Happened To Common Sense?* she stated:

> The objective, clearly enunciated by the leaders of UNCED, is to bring about a change in the present system of independent nations. The future is to be world government, with central planning by the UN. Fear of environmental crises, whether real or not, is expected to lead to compliance. If force is needed, it will be provided by a UN green-helmeted police force, already authorized by the Security Council.[6]

Out of this conference came the Global Climate Change Treaty which was signed by President Bush and ratified by the U. S. Senate on October 15, 1992. This United Nations treaty, moving us closer to world government, was based upon the theory of global warming.

One of the disconcerting things about the theory of Global Warming was the lack of professional consultation upon the part of leaders of the Earth Summit. Dixie Lee Ray had this to say about the concern of leading world scientists:

> In contrast to the predictions of impending ecological doom from Strong, Bruntland, and other UN leaders of the Earth Summit, more than 250 of the world's leading scientists, including 27 Nobel laureates, released a statement on June 1, 1992, called the Heidelberg Appeal. It was directed to the heads of state that were attending the Rio Conference and appealed for the use of common sense and reliable science in making recommendations for action on environmental problems. As background, the scientists pointed out that it is neither reasonable nor prudent for major political decisions to be based on presumptions about issues in science, which, in the current state of knowledge, are still only hypotheses. They pointed out that in the more than two years of preparation for the Earth Summit, there was no significant involvement of scientists who specialize in the specific problem areas under consideration, nor were the competent scientists even informed.[7]

Dixie Lee Ray went on to add this comment:

> Unfortunately, this appeal was neither acknowledged nor considered at the Earth Summit. All of the actions taken there were without the benefit of competent

scientific input. By every measure the conference represented a signal victory for the foes of scientific progress, knowledge, and economic development.[8]

The truth is that this UN grab for global dictatorship is based upon a myth. In 100 years of measuring the net change in temperature over the earth no more than one half of one degree Centigrade has been recorded. Added to the proof of those measurements is the data from Tiros II, a temperature-measuring satellite that has orbited the earth since 1978. This data shows no significant temperature trend, either up or down. Outside of instrument-measured variations, records go back as far as 1,700 years to show that climate varies naturally outside of any man made cause.

For those who desire more information about this and many other vital environmental issues, we recommend Dixy Lee Ray's book *Environmental Overkill: Whatever Happened To Common Sense?* published by Regnery Gateway, Washington, D. C.

Another example of a theory based upon propaganda and half-truths is ozone depletion. Based upon this theory, laws have already been passed by the U. S. Congress that will, by 1995, ban the manufacture of chlorofluorocarbons (CFCs). This action came about as a result of another UN treaty referred to as the "Montreal Protocol on Substances that Deplete the Ozone Layer." Under the provisions of this treaty, Americans can be fined $25,000 per day and imprisoned for five years.

Non-toxic CFC (freon) is used in every refrigeration unit in America. It is also used in firefighting. Unless a substitute is developed, its ban will mean that eventually every refrigeration unit in America, and the world, will have to be replaced. As portrayed by Dixy Lee Ray, the cost in money and human suffering will be astronomical:

> If one adds up all the estimated costs from the different affected industries, it may be as high as $5 trillion worldwide by the year 2005. Because of the severe effect on transportation and storage of food due to the loss or greatly increased cost of refrigeration, estimates indicate that between 20 to 40 million people will die yearly from hunger, starvation, and food-borne diseases.[9]

While ozone does vary, there is no scientific evidence to prove that it is being permanently depleted because of CFCs, nor is there any scientific evidence, based upon the necessary long term measurements, to prove there is a problem of ozone depletion at all. As to CFCs being involved in ozone depletion Dixy Lee Ray had this to say:

> How does CFC rise when its molecules are four to eight times heavier than air? All experience with freon and related CFCs shows that they are non-volatile and so heavy that you can pour CFCs from a container and if some of them spill, they will collect at the lowest point on the ground where soil bacteria will decompose them.[10]

Honest studies show that the highest percentage of chloride in the atmosphere is caused by nature and is outside of the control of man. According to Dixy Lee Ray:

> When Mount Tambora in Indonesia erupted in 1813, it ejected 211 million tons of chloride. At the highest rate of worldwide CFC production, it would have taken 282 years to produce as much chloride-yielding CFCs as this one eruption.
>
> Although measurments of chloride are not available for many modern volcanic eruptions, we know that Mount Erebus in Anarctica has been producing 1,000 tons of chloride daily since 1972. Mount Erebus is located 10 kilometers upwind of McMurdo Sound, where ozone measurements are made. The volcano pumps out 50 times more chloride annually than an entire year's production of CFCs.[11]

Global Warming and Ozone Depletion are only two examples of unproven theories being used as an excuse for members of the United States Senate to ratify treaties that nulify the Constitution they have sworn to uphold. UN treaties already being proposed will, if ratified, place the American people under the rule of a one world government.

The great tragedy is that the average American is unaware that this is happening. The majority have no idea who the representatives are, often ones they have elected, that are voting them into slavery. Fortunately, this information is available.

For a reliable up-to-date source of information on these and a host of other vital issues we recommend that our readers subscribe to *The New American* magazine. It is published bi-weekly and is available from, The New American, P.O. Box 8040, Appleton, Wisconsin.

A good answer to the "doomsdayers" is found in the Old Testament Scriptures. It is embodied in a promise given by the Creator immediately after the universal flood had ended and Noah was able to exit the Ark.

> And Noah builded an altar unto the Lord; and took of every clean beast, and of every clean foul, and offered burnt offerings on the altar.
>
> And the Lord smelled a sweet savour; and the Lord said in his heart, I will not again curse the ground any more for man's sake; for the imagination of man's heart is evil from his youth; neither will I again smite any more every thing living , as I have done.
>
> While the earth remaineth, seedtime and harvest, and cold and heat, and summer and winter, and day and night shall not cease.
>
> Genesis 8:20-22

Chapter 13

A New Movement In History

And they that be wise shall shine as the brightness of the firmament; and they that turn many to righteousness as the stars for ever and ever,

Daniel 12:3

And ye shall know the truth, and the truth shall make you free.

John 8:32

Following World War II, there were many prominent Americans who tried to warn the American people that their government was betraying nation after nation into Communist hands. Many of these men were in government where they had witnessed these betrayals first hand. When they tried to speak out they found themselves ignored and harassed, and, in some cases, the victims of a smear campaign. Some died under mysterious circumstances, as did James Forrestal, U. S. Secretary of War, who was a member of the CFR, but began opposing their plans.

Another example was Arthur Bliss Lane, U. S. Ambassador to Poland. Ambassador Lane was greatly alarmed as he witnessed the betrayal of Poland into Communist hands by his own State Department. He resigned as Ambassador and wrote a book entitled *I Saw Poland Betrayed* to warn the American people of the extent to which the U. S. Government was aiding the Communist conquest of other nations. His book was such a shocking revelation that it should have been a national best seller. Instead, it was so effectively suppressed that only a few copies were sold. Ambassador Lane was so devastated that he died a broken man, believing there was no hope for his country.

But for the efforts of one man, who refused to accept defeat of his country by a powerful conspiracy, very few people would ever have heard of Ambassadors Lane's book or dozens of similar ones exposing the conspiracy. Realizing the impossibility of reaching the American people through the CFR-controlled news media, this American businessman set out to build an organization to circumvent the almost total control of public opinion in the United States. Few men could have been better qualified to be the founder of such an organization.

Born in a rural setting in 1899, his school teacher mother started his education when he was only two years old. At three he was proficient at reading, at four had memorized the multiplication tables, and at six was adept at algebra. At seven he started reading Latin and read all nine volumes of Ridpath's *History of the World.* He entered high school at the age of ten, and the University of North Carolina at the age of twelve, graduating in the top third of his class when he was only sixteen. He later attended the U. S. Naval Academy for two years, ranking fourth in a class of almost a thousand. He then entered Harvard Law School for two and a half years.

Much of the wisdom and insight of this gifted individual resulted from his determined pursuit of knowledge. His book *The Romance Of Education* dealt with such diverse fields as language, history, mathematics, and poetry, all subjects in which he had excelled. His personal library grew to contain 5,000 volumes, most of which he had read. After rising to national prominence as a successful businessman, he laid aside his business responsibilities to devote his life to bringing the truth to the American people.

And so it was that on December 9, 1958, Robert Welch met with 11 other prominent men in a two day meeting which resulted in the founding of The John Birch Society. This meeting that took place in Indianapolis, Indiana, began a new movement in history. Outside of religious groups, this was the first time a major organization was ever created for the sole purpose of using truth as a weapon against evil. The motto of The John Birch Society (JBS) was expressed in this manner by its founder: "Education is our total strategy and truth is our only weapon."[1]

As a result of the founding of the JBS, the manipulators of public opinion faced something they had never faced before. It soon became evident to them that the JBS understood exactly what they were up to, and knew how to use the one weapon they could not stand against. That weapon was simply *truth*.

In 1966, Mr. Welch made a famous speech called "The Truth In Time" that struck at the very heart of the activities of the manipulators. In this speech, he concluded that there was a Master Conspiracy above the Communists that had brought them to power, and that this Master Conspiracy was made up of the super-wealthy.

In 1983 JBS staff member John F. McManus wrote a book about these powerful men entitled *The Insiders*. In a radio interview, Mr. McManus explained why he chose this title for his book:

> The title *The Insiders* was borrowed from Robert Welch, who, back in 1965, posited a theory that the world was in the grip of international financiers, politicians, etc., who were not themselves Communists, but were in fact above the Communists.
>
> These were the people who finance Communism, help it, dignify it, keep it going. . . . These people themselves weren't Communist, but were part of a conspiracy that had actually brought Communism into existence back in the middle of the 1800s, and were keeping it in existence today, and were using Communism to take over nation after nation on the route toward a world government. Robert Welch called these powerful individuals, "The Insiders."[2]

As a result of the leadership of Robert Welch and the Council of The John Birch Society, the Society soon attracted tens of thousands of dedicated members throughout the United States. The truth about the

Insiders began to roll off the press in books and articles, some being sold in the millions. Audio tapes and videos were produced and distributed across the country. Bookstores were opened and a national speakers bureau was established. From the standpoint of the Insiders, something had to be done.

Since the Insiders could not refute the truth being told about them, they launched the most massive smear campaign that had ever been experienced by any private group in the United States. The CFR-controlled news media spearheaded the attack, spreading misinformation, and outright lies about the JBS on a daily basis. The attacks slowed down but never stopped the Society. Years later at the 35th anniversary celebration of the JBS in Indianapolis, Indiana, long time staff member Thomas Hill gave this account of the efforts to destroy the JBS:

> Thirty-five years ago in this city called Indianapolis, eleven men gathered to hear what another man was prepared to tell them. Thirty-two years ago, most of the National and International Press, political leaders in the federal government as well as political leaders in many state governments, liberal and pro-communist pundits from one coast to another, and a host of hacks and assorted opportunists of every conceivable description, assured their readers, and all who would listen, that this scourge of the country, this semi-secret, fanatical and undemocratic monstrosity known as The John Birch Society, would soon be relegated into obscurity.
>
> In 1968, some seven years later, The John Birch Society celebrated the 10th anniversary of its founding.

And still the chorus of the above mentioned collection of collectivists continued to predict the downfall of the organization. Fifteen years later the Society celebrated its 25th Anniversary and Robert Welch would be presented the keys to the city of Indianapolis.

And now, 35 years have passed by, the last nine without the presence of our founder. This organization which has suffered such vilification as no other, certainly in this century, had not only survived, but in the process has provided solid information, direction, hope and encouragement to millions and millions of our countrymen. What is more, its goals remain the same; and its principles, and organizational body are intact. Perhaps the single most important reason why the Society is alive and well today, is because sufficient numbers of its members went to the trouble of reaching others with enough information, rather than too little.[3]

One of the reasons the JBS influenced millions was that it was far more than just an anti-communist organization. Its leadership and members understood the real basis of the struggle going on in the world. Society spokesman, G. Edward Griffin, explains this struggle and what is necessary to defeat it:

The war raging around the world today is not between communists and anti-communists. As words are misleading, a better word to use to describe the forces here is the forces of collectivism verses the forces of individualism.

A collectivist is a person who believes that the collective is more important than the individual, that the group is more important than the individual, and the individual must be sacrificed if necessary, for, and this is the phrase that you have heard so many times, "for the greater good of the greater number." Basically, the collectivist believes that the individual is not responsible for his own welfare, that it is the responsibility of the group to take care of him. That means, of course, the State.

The individualist, on the other hand, believes that the individual is the most important element in society, and that any doctrine which ignores the individual's rights is a false doctrine. The individualist also believes in doing things for himself, in having as little government as possible, so that the individual is responsible for himself, his family and his loved ones.

If we were just facing the philosophy of Marxism, then we could easily defeat it with the philosophy of freedom. If we were just fighting against the concept of Collectivism, we could easily defeat it with the superior ideology of Individualism. But that's not what we are facing. We're facing the combination of ideology and organization. We're facing a well-disciplined literally worldwide army of people who have leaders, follow directions, take orders, and work in unison to accomplish targeted goals. The only way that we who want to preserve our freedom can oppose that, and defeat it, is not only with just a superior ideology of individualism, but we must also have a superior, or at least an equally efficient organization to oppose their organization.[4]

This understanding of the basic nature of the struggle between Collectivism and Individualism easily enabled members of the JBS to identify the enemies of freedom. These enemies always work for more government, less responsibility, and use amorality (lack of conscience) as a means to accomplish their goals. In contrast, the goal of the JBS is less government, more responsibility, and a better world based upon faith-inspired morality.

The thing about the JBS that worried the Master Conspiracy even more than its philosophy, was the potential inherent in its organization. For here was an organization that could not be infiltrated, misdirected, or destroyed by smear tactics. Here was an organization that knew its enemy and that enemy's weaknesses. The conspirators knew that if the JBS could attract sufficient membership, their game would be over. Consequently, their greatest efforts were aimed at preventing this from happening.

The young man for whom the Society is named was a Christian Missionary to China named John Birch. John became a legend in his own time while serving under General Claire Chennault, Commander of the famous Flying Tigers. Under Chennault, John Birch rose to the rank of U. S. Army Captain and served as an intelligence officer behind enemy lines, earning the title of "the eyes and ears of the 14th Air Force." It was John Birch who helped General Jimmy Doolittle get out of China after his famous raid on Tokyo in 1942.

John had planned to remain in China after the war and carry on his missionary work, but his life was cut short by his murder in August 1945 at the hands of Chinese Communist guerrillas, just a few days after the end of World War II.

The amazing story of the life of John Birch and the United States government's cover up of his murder was written in James and Marti Hefley's book *The Secret File On John Birch*. The book was published in 1980 by Tyndale House Publishers, Inc., Wheaton, Illinois. In the foreword the authors stated:

> Government bureaucracy and political pressure served to keep many of the facts secret for many years, particularly the truth about his murder by Chinese Communists. The complete story of his life can now be told for the first time, thanks to declassification of essential documents.[5]

One American who had first hand knowledge of the Communist murder of John Birch, and who was himself victimized by political intrigue in Washington, was Lieutenant William Miller who was also an intelligence officer in China at the time of John's death. It was William Miller who buried John Birch. Following is part of his eyewitness account given at the 35th anniversary celebration of The John Birch Society:

> But I would like to cover some points on John Birch and his background, and also the background of the whole affair in Washington that involved me after I buried John Birch in China.
> . . . While serving with the military intelligence service in China in 1945, I was privileged to become a close friend of a legendary intelligence agent I had admired from afar, but was only able to know and work

with during the last four months of his tragically short life. Thus, his last-minute loss of life to the habitually murderous Communists was a traumatic event for me.

Let us never forget that John was in a sense a victim of our own American liberal conspiracy, naive or otherwise, to deliberately sabotage the pro-Christian and pro-American Nationalist Government of China by every propaganda and logistical means at its disposal.

In other words, had the Communist leadership in China not been encouraged by irresponsible or ideologically mischievous Americans both in China and in Washington, to consider their agrarian reform the wave of the future for China, no Communist leader in China would have dared arrest, let alone brutally murder in cold blood, an American Officer on any official mission.

So when I returned to the Pentagon by air in November 1945, I was not surprised to find John's death an official nonevent. It was as if he had simply been hit by a stray bullet, and that was the end of that. Furthermore, my official report to General Alfred Wedemeyer telling the whole story of the murder . . . had been classified secret and filed away accordingly.

Later as an officer in the State Department Liaison Bureau of the Military Intelligence Service in Washington, I was saddened to witness, from within the system, how leftist intrigue to destroy the Nationalist credibility reached into Congress to poison many fair-minded men. In fact, years later in 1951, when I finally told Senator Knowland about my original report to China Theater Headquarters on Captain Birch's murder by a Communist Regimental Commander, he was furious, and went on the floor as Senate Majority Leader to state categorically that had he known of the atrocity in time, it would have changed the whole course of American Foreign Policy towards the Communists in China. And in consequence of this change in policy, the United States would have been spared fighting two wars, one in Korea, and one in Vietnam.[6]

Many events on the secret side of history have greatly affected the destinies of men to varying degrees, but no other known single conspiratorial accomplishment has ever affected so many human beings as the cover-up of the communists' murder of John Birch. For, had the truth been known in time, the 500 million people then living in China could not have been betrayed into slavery nor would 60 million have been murdered by the Communists. This realization was one of the motivating factors that caused Robert Welch to found The John Birch Society.

Just as the circumstances of the death of John Birch had such far reaching consequences, the inspiration of his life also had far reaching consequences, resulting in his name being known throughout the civilized world. Because of the work of the Society which bears his name, the final results of the life of John Birch are yet to be recorded.

For more information about The John Birch Society write to, The John Birch Society, P. O. Box 8040, Appleton, Winconsin.

Chapter 14

The Soul of Babylon

> And there came one of the seven angels which had the seven vials, and talked with me, saying unto me, Come hither; I will shew unto thee the judgement of the great whore that sitteth upon many waters.
>
> With whom the kings of the earth have committed fornication, and the inhabitants of the earth have been made drunk with the wine of her fornication.
>
> Revelation 17:1 &2

As the Prophet Isaiah gives us a picture of the soul of Ancient Babylon, the Apostle John gives us a picture of the soul of Mystery Babylon. John's description of the inner workings of Mystery Babylon is also an amazing parallel to Modern Day Babylon.

The use of sorceries is one of the evils attributed to Babylon, "for by thy sorceries were all nations deceived" Rev. 18:23. *The American Heritage Dictionary* defines sorcery as, "The use of supernatural power over others through the assistance of evil spirits; witchcraft; black magic."

According to *Strong's Greek Dictionary of the New Testament*, the word for sorceries used in Rev. 18:23 is a Greek word φαρμακεία (pharmakêia) from which we get the word for pharmacy. The root word is φάρμακον (pharmakŏn) and can mean a drug or spell-giving potion.[1]

Illegal drug use, one of the most important issues of our time, has been highly publicized on one hand and covered up on the other. While the problem has been publicized, much of the truth about the cause has been covered up or ignored.

A well documented source of information on this subject is Joseph D. Douglass, Jr.'s book *Red Cocaine: The Drugging of America.* Dr. Ray S. Cline, former Deputy Director for Intelligence, of the Central Intelligence Agency, had this to say about *Red Cocaine:*

> Dr. Joseph Douglass, the author of this book , is not selling a theory but instead calling attention to evidence. He has marshalled his facts carefully, presents them responsibly and cautiously, and offers a wealth of soberly documented data. That data describes in detail the efforts of China, the Soviet Union, and its many surrogates, to use drugs over many decades as weapons designed to damage and weaken — if not destroy — the stability of Free World countries. The top target is and always has been, of course, the United States.[2]

Cline also had this to say about a coverup of information about the major source of the drug problem:

> If we are serious about winning this war on drugs, we must know, too, to what extent it is true — as this book argues — that top officials in our government have had access to this evidence for many years, but preferred

to hush it up out of concern for what public disclosure would do to U. S.-Sino/Soviet relations.

Data that does not support the politically - desired (or fashionable) goal of managing détente between Moscow and Washington has a hard time — a very hard time — surfacing or being heard. Needless to say, throughout the intelligence community, scores of conscientious officers fight against this pernicious process, often to the extent of putting their jobs, reputations, and very careers on the line.[3]

Much of the evidence presented in *Red Cocaine* was revealed by Jan Sejna, who defected from Czechoslovakia to the United states in February 1968. According to Douglass, "Sejna was a top-level, decision making party official. He met regularly with the highest officials in the Soviet Union and other communist countries. He was present during the inception, planning, and implementation of Soviet narcotics trafficking operations."[4] Douglass went on to relate how efforts were made in Washington to sidetrack Sejna and ignore his information.

The plans laid out by the Soviets were so thorough and extensive that they included the establishment of training schools for drug distributors, clinics to study the effects of drugs, and laboratories to research new drugs. In 1955 the Soviets decided to infiltrate organized crime throughout the world and use it as a covert mechanism for distributing drugs. [5]

Sejna explained why American youth was the main target in the Soviet drug war:

> But the focus for significant change had to be the young generation. These were the people that we needed to work on to change the military, to retard scientific development, and to influence the government leadership. This is why the American youth were the primary target for the drugs.[6]

That the flow of drugs into this country has not abated is a sure indication that nothing has changed regarding the long-range plans of the Soviets. For those of our readers who are concerned enough to look further into the deliberate drug warfare against America, Joseph Douglass' 277 page book *Red Cocaine: The Drugging of America* is available from American Opinion Book Service, P. O. Box 8040, Appleton, Wisconsin.

As mentioned in chapter 9, the word "fornication" used in describing Mystery Babylon has two meanings. As used in Scripture, when applied to individuals it meant sexual immorality. When applied to rulers and nations it meant idolatry. According to *Strong's Greek Dictionary of the New Testament*, the words used for fornication in John's description of Mystery Babylon (πορνεία por-ni'-ah and πορνεύω porn-yoó-o) literally mean adultery but figuratively mean idolatry.[7] Both terms certainly describe Modern Day Babylon, the most significant of which is idolatry. Due to the New Age Movement, no time in history has seen such a wide spread acceptance of the heathen religious practice of idolatry. The main center of power and influence for this movement is that modern Tower of Babel called the United Nations. One UN report, *The New International Economic Order: A Spiritual Imperative,* proclaimed, "The work of the U. N. is indeed spiritual and holds profound import for the future of civilization."[8] William Jasper had this to say about the religious nature of the United Nations:

> The UN, along with its programs and policies, is becoming ever more worthy of comparison to the Tower of Babel, as rampant idolatry and militant paganism thoroughly permeate the organization.
>
> The United Nations is steadily becoming the center of a syncretic new world religion, a weird and diabolical convergence of New Age mysticism, pantheism, aboriginal animism, atheism, communism, socialism, Luciferian occultism, apostate Christianity, Islam, Taoism, Buddhism, and Hinduism. The devotees and apostles of this new faith include the kind of strange admixture of crystal worshipers, astrologers, radical femisists, environmentalists, cabalists, human potentialists, Eastern mystics, pop psychologists, and "liberal" clergymen one would normally tend to associate with the off-beat, sandals-and-beads counterculture of the 1960s. But today's worshipers in this rapidly expanding movement are as likely to be scientists, diplomats, corporate presidents, heads of state, international bankers, and leaders of mainstream Christian churches.[9]

The leaders of this "new world religion" referred to by William Jasper, reject the Bible and all religious teaching that admits God as creator. They reject the monotheistic (one God) concept as taught by Christianity, Islam, and Judaism and embrace pantheism believing that god is an impersonal force that pervades all things. Since god pervades all things, the universe, rocks, trees, animals, humans, etc. are "God."

In this pagan view, since man is not the creation of God, he is not accountable to Him nor do his rights and responsibilities come from God. This is similar to Old Testament history during the time of Samson when "every man did that which was right in his own eyes" Judges 17:6.

Reverend Clarence Kelly, in his book *Conspiracy Against God And Man* explained this about pantheism:

> Pantheism is a favorite doctrine of collectivists, because . . . it offers a concept of man which, on religious grounds, subordinates the individual to the collective. It also functions as an effective tool in the subversion of God-centered religion by making religion man-centered, and thereby giving a religious sanction to the doctrines and programs of political collectivism. At the same time, pantheism can be used as a stage in bringing people from theism to atheistic materialism.
>
> Weishaupt appreciated the destructive value of pantheism, and devised a scheme for the creation of a new substitute religion incorporating naturalistic doctrines. . . . Under cover of his declamations of concern for reason, truth, humanity, liberty, and original

equality, he planted the age-old doctrines of pantheism. He portrayed his new "Christianity" as being apostolic and original, a "Christianity" that institutionalized religion has obscured. The technique is similar to the one used by certain modern theologians who claim to have uncovered the "real" meaning of the scriptures.[10]

The roots of the UN new world religion go back to the teaching of Helena Petrovna Blavatsky (1831-1891) who founded the Theosophical Society in New York in 1875. Blavatsky turned Bible teaching upside down and taught that Satan was the victim of Jehovah. She taught that, "Satan, the Serpent of Genesis, is the real creator and benefactor, the Father of Spiritual mankind. For it is he . . . who opened the eyes of the automaton (Adam) created by Jehovah, . . ."[11]

After Blavatsky's death in 1891, the leadership of the world-wide Theosophical Society fell to Annie Besant, who added volumes of occultic writings to those of Blavatsky.

Besant was followed by Alice Bailey, who with her husband, Foster Bailey, constructed much of the foundation of the New Age religion. Openly showing their preference for a Satanic religion they launched Lucifer Publishing Company which published the theosophical periodical *Lucifer.* In 1922, the Baileys established the Lucis Trust which now serves as an umbrella organization for a number of globalist New Age occult organizations.

According to Lucis Trust, one of these organizations, World Goodwill, is represented at regular United Nation briefing sessions in New York. Regular weekly radio broadcasts of talks given at World Goodwill meetings are beamed by shortwave to a world wide audience. Their "plan" is to establish a "spiritual Hierarchy of the planet."[12]

One of the most influential persons guiding the United Nations unfolding "spirituality" is Maurice Strong who has been referred to by his followers as "the custodian of the planet." Strong's goal is to alter the history of the world.[13]

In her book *The Hidden Dangers Of The Rainbow: The New Age Movement and Our Coming Age of Barbarism* Constance Cumbey has this to say about the New Age Movement:

> According to New Age sources, the New Age Movement is a worldwide network. It consists of tens of thousands of cooperating organizations. Their primary goal or the secret behind their "unity-in-diversity" is the formation of a "New World Order." The Movement usually operates on the basis of a well-formulated body of underlying esoteric or occult teachings.
>
> The glue binding most New Age devotees is one of common mystical experiences. "Experiential religion" is considered vital within the Movement. A substantial proportion of those within the Movement strongly believe in psychic phenomena and say they do so because of "direct experiences."[14]

As to the attitude of the New Age Movement toward other religious groups Cumbey states:

> While professing support for religious liberty in their public releases, the Alice Bailey books which are meticulously followed within the Movement call for complete abridgement of this freedom. They openly and boldly set forth plans for a new mandatory world religion — a religion completely breaking with the concept of Jesus as the Christ and God as the Father. Jews and Christians — Roman Catholic and Protestant alike — as well as uncooperative Moslems are openly slated for persecution and even a "cleansing action" should they fail to cooperate.[15]

Cumbey goes on to state that, "millions have been deceived into supporting projects designed to eventually strip even themselves of their civil liberties, much of their property, their preferred religion, and perhaps even their lives."[16]

In his book *Global Tyranny . . . Step By Step* William Jasper explained that the hierarchy of Hitler's Nazi movement, "were ardent theosophists and their esoteric societies . . . were steeped in the same occultism and pantheism so prevalent in today's New Age and environmental movements."[17] He went on to warn:

> Today, all people of good will recognize the diabolically evil nature of the *Fuehrer's* failed regime. What is now desperately needed is a widespread recognition of the fact that the neo-pagan,

internationalist-socialist new world order being promoted by and through the United Nations is as militantly anti-Christian, as malevolently totalitarian, and as satanically evil as that jackbooted tyranny of our recent past.

This time, its headquarters is not in Berlin, but in New York City.[18]

Just how far UN leaders may plan to go in their pantheistic role as "custodians of the earth" was revealed in an interview with the *UNESCO Courier* for November 1991 by Jacques Cousteau the famed oceanographer:

> The damage people cause to the planet is a function of demographics — it is equal to the degree of development. One American burdens the earth much more than twenty Bangaladeshes. The damage is directly linked to consumption. Our society is turning toward more and more needless consumption. It is a vicious circle that I compare to cancer. . . .
>
> *This is a terrible thing to say. In order to stabilize world population, we must eliminate 350,000 people per day. It is a horrible thing to say, but it's just as bad not to say it* [emphasis added].[19]

Throughout the Old and New Testament scripture the true purpose of creation is reiterated beginning in Genesis 1:27 & 28:

> So God created man in his own image, in the image of God created he him; male and female created he them.

And God blessed them, and God said unto them, Be fruitful, and multiply, and replenish the earth, and subdue it: and have dominion over the fish of the sea, and over the fowl of the air, and over every living thing that moveth upon the earth.

The Prophet Isaiah delivered a sobering message for those who wish to banish God and rule in His place. It was a message referring to Lucifer and directed to Ancient Babylon. It may also have been intended for the rulers of a Modern Day Babylon. Here are Isaiah's words:

How art thou fallen from heaven, O Lucifer, son of the morning! how art thou cut down to the ground, which did weaken the nations!

For thou hast said in thine heart, I will ascend into heaven, I will exalt my throne above the stars of God: I will sit also upon the mount of the congregation, in the sides of the north:

I will ascend above the heights of the clouds; I will be like the most High.

Yet thou shalt be brought down to hell, to the sides of the pit.

Isaiah 14:12 - 15

Chapter 15

The Fall of Babylon

> And they cast dust on their heads, and cried, weeping and wailing, saying, Alas, alas, that great city, wherein were made rich all that had ships in the sea by reason of her costliness! for in one hour is she made desolate.
> Revelation 18:19

During the 20th century, there has been established a center of world power possessing all of the major attributes of the "Mystery Babylon" described in the Book of Revelation. This center of world power can be viewed not in the future tense, but in the present. In other words, it exists now.

This Modern Day Babylon qualifies to be labeled as "Mystery" (secret) because one of its most successful accomplishments has been to keep its existence unknown to very few outside of its circle of participants. This element of secrecy has enabled this Modern Day Babylon to use its influence over the U. S. Government as a means of extending its power throughout the world.

While the CFR is the organization most identifiable as the agency of this influence over the U. S. Government, it is not the only one, nor is the CFR the top level of the Master Conspiracy.

Whether or not this Modern Day Babylon is a direct

descendant of the Illuminati, no one on the outside knows. At the very least, it is probable that its leaders use the organizational structure of the Illuminati. It is certainly evident that this satanically-inspired conspiracy has followed the Illuminati's plan to destroy all religion, overthrow all governments, and rule the world.

Is this Modern Day Babylon indeed the Mystery Babylon described in the Book of Revelation? No matter what our personal conclusions may be, this is a question that time alone can answer.

The Scriptures record that the rule of Ancient Babylon came to a sudden and unexpected end. They also record that the extensive power of Mystery Babylon comes to a sudden, unexpected, and tragic end. The fall of Mystery Babylon is announced over seven times. The "death, and mourning, and famine" that she caused for others is doubled to her and Mystery Babylon falls, never to rise again.

The Scripture makes it plain that believers must have no part in such an evil structure as Mystery Babylon. This surely applies to any Modern Day Babylon as well. The action required to accomplish this was summed up by William Jasper:

> As late as the hour has become, it is still not too late to avert catastrophe and save our freedom. The world's future need not degenerate into what George Orwell wrote would resemble "a boot stamping on a human face — forever!" But the urgency of our situation cannot be overstated. Simply put, unless significant numbers of

Americans can be awakened from their slumbers, shaken from their apathy and ignorance, pulled away from their diversions, and convinced to work, pray, vote, speak up, struggle, and fight against the powers arrayed against them, then such a horrible fate surely awaits all of us.[1]

Thus far, the greatest tragedy is not only that we have been losing a world-wide battle for the minds and souls of men, but that the majority of the good people in America — have never even been in the battle. Babylons eventually always fall. We still have a choice whether we separate ourselves, and our nation, from our Modern Day Babylon — or fall with it.

Chapter 16

Conclusions

And I heard another voice from heaven, saying,
Come out of her, my people, that ye be not partakers of
her sins, and that ye receive not of her plagues.
Revelation 18:4

Throughout history, man's attitude toward government has often stood in the way of material and spiritual progress. Good people struggling against evil have more often than not failed to win the upper hand because they did not see the big picture, especially as it applied to the proper role of government. America was a great nation for 100 years because our Founding Fathers understood this, and gave us a Constitutional Republic that limited the power, size, and scope of government.

The proper role of government was explained very well over 150 years ago by a member of the French Legislative Assembly, Frederic Bastiat, (1801-1850). Writing just prior to and after the French Revolution of 1848 (the third revolution), and basing his arguments against socialism on the evidence of the devastation socialism brought to his own country, Bastiat admonished his colleagues not to repeat past mistakes.

Although most of his countrymen ignored his logic, the truths that he presented were so eternal that hundreds of thousands of copies of Baistiat's work *The Law*, first published as a pamphlet in June, 1850, are still in existence and used today. In *The Law* Bastiat explained the proper basis of law as:

> Life, faculties, production — in other words, individuality, liberty, property — this is man. And in spite of the cunning of artful political leaders, these three gifts from God precede all human legislation, and are superior to it.
>
> Life, liberty, and property do not exist because men have made laws. On the contrary, it was the fact that life, liberty, and property existed beforehand that caused men to make laws in the first place.
>
> What, then, is law? It is the collective organization of the individual right to lawful defense.[1]

Bastiat went on to explain how the law (government) should be used:

> The law is the organization of the natural right of lawful defense. It is the substitution of a common force for individual forces. And this common force is to do only what the individual forces have a natural and lawful right to do: to protect persons, liberties, and properties; to maintain the right of each, and to cause *justice* to reign over us all.[2]

In essence, what Bastiat is saying is that the moral standard for government is the same as the moral standard for individuals. In other words, if it is wrong for individuals to steal, lie, murder, etc., it is also morally wrong for government to do so. It is unfortunate that evils of every sort are tolerated as long as they are done in the name of government. Bastiat went at length to explain that legalized plunder (redistribution of wealth) is always a perversion of the proper function of the law and eventually leads to moral degradation, civil discontent, and revolution.

Bastiat summed up his arguments in this manner:

> Which countries contain the most peaceful, the most moral, and the happiest people? Those people are found in the countries where the law least interferes with private affairs; where government is least felt; where the individual has the greatest scope, and free opinion the greatest influence; where the administrative powers are fewest and simplest; . . . where the inventions of men are most nearly in harmony with the laws of God; in short, the happiest, most moral, and most peaceful people are those who most nearly follow this principle. . . . [3]

These principles, as embodied in the United States Constitution, were such a roadblock to the establishment of a New World Order that the Master Conspiracy could have made little progress without, first changing, and then subverting it. It is still such an important factor in the world-wide struggle between good and evil, that if the U. S. Constitution was restored to its proper place as the law of the land today, Modern Day Babylon would fall tomorrow. Along with its fall would go many of the ills that plague our nation, most of which are due to the erosion of the Constitution.

The answer to the great danger posed by the New World Order is for the United States to get out of the United Nations, and restore the U. S. Constitution as the law of the land.

To accomplish this, the American people must elect representatives to Congress (especially the House of Representatives) that are statesmen and not politicians, the measuring stick being their Constitutional voting records and not their rhetoric. A simple majority of men and women in Congress who will use the Constitution as a basis for all legislation, and appropriations, can restore the Republic.

Due to the Insiders' control over the opinion molding media in the United States, the understanding necessary to accomplish this will have to be created by a grass roots movement of the people themselves. Fortunately, this movement has already been established and all of the necessary educational tools are available. The only missing element is enough concerned citizens to use *truth* as a weapon to overcome the daily barrage of falsehoods that are now being showered upon the American people.

No one knows what all may transpire during the struggle that we must face. One thing is certain, to compromise with the forces of darkness is to lose, for any victory on the side of evil is only temporary. This was expressed by Jesus in Mark 8:36 when He said, "For what shall it profit a man, if he shall gain the whole world, and lose his own soul?" King Solomon expressed the same thing in this manner, "Let us hear the conclusion of the whole matter: Fear God, and keep his commandments: for this is the whole duty of man. For God shall bring every work into judgement, with every secret thing, whether it be good, or whether it be evil." Ecclesiastes 12:13 & 14.

Footnotes

Chapter 1. Ancient Babylon

1. Henry H. Halley, *Halley's Bible Handbook* (Grand Rapids, MI: Zondervan Publishing House, 1989), p. 344.

Chapter 4. Secret Societies

1. Nesta H. Webster, *Secret Societies and Subversive Movements* (Christian Book Club of America, 1986), p. 3.
2. John Robison, *Proofs of a Conspiracy* (Appleton, WI: Western Islands, 1967), p. 268
3. Webster, p. 64.
4. Ibid., p. 39.

Chapter 5. The Illuminati

1. Nester H. Webster, *Secret Societies and Subversive Movements* (Christian Book Club of America, 1986), p. 220.
2. John Robison, *Proofs of a Conspiracy* (Appleton, WI: Western Islands, 1967), p.111.
3. Webster, p. 222-223.
4. Robison, p. 112.
5. Ibid., p. 109.
6. Ibid., p. 86
7. Ibid., p. 81.
8. Ibid., p. 94.
9. Ibid., p. 114
10. Ibid., p. 115
11. Ibid., p. 113.

Chapter 6. The French Revolution

1. Nesta H. Webster, *The French Revolution* (Costa Mesa, CA: The Noontide Press, 1992), p. v.
2. Ibid., p. ix.
3. Ibid., p. ix.
4. Ibid., p. 6-7.
5. Ibid., p. 8.
6. Ibid., p. 191.
7. William P. Hoar, *Architects of Conspiracy (Appleton, WI:* Western Islands, 1984), p. 1.
8. Ibid., p. 2
9. Webster, p. 294.

10. Ibid., p. 331.
11. Ibid., p. 431.
12. Ibid., p. 432.
13 John Robison, *Proofs of a Conspiracy* (Appleton, WI: Western Islands, 1967), p. 245.
14 Webster, p. 428-429
15. Robison, p. 260.
16. Webster, p. 487.

Chapter 7. The American Republic

1. John Eidsmoe, *Christianity And The Constitution: The Faith of Our Founding Fathers* (Grand Rapids, MI: Baker Book House, 1987), p. 208.
2. Ibid., p. 22.
3. Ibid., p. 22.
4. Henry Grady Weaver, *The Mainspring of Human Progress* (Irvington-On-Hudson, New York: The Foundation for Economic Education, Inc., 1984), p. 65
5. Ibid., p. 67-68.
6. Robert Welch, "Republics and Democracies," American Opinion Reprint Series, (Appleton, WI: The John Birch Society, 1970), p. 19.

7. Ibid., p. 19.
8. Ibid., p. 19-20.
9. Ibid., p. 27.

Chapter 8. Attempts to Divide America

1. William P. Hoar, *Architects Of Conspiracy: An Intriguing History* (Appleton, WI: Western Islands, 1984), p. 10.
2. William H. McIlhany, *Journal of Individualist Studies Vol. 1, No. 2* (Beverly Hills, CA: Individualist Research Foundation, 1992), p. 3.
3. Hoar, p. 12.

Chapter 10. Building Modern Babylon

1. James Perloff, *The Shadows of Power: The Council on Foreign Relations and the American Decline* (Appleton, WI: Western Islands, 1990), p. 23.
2. Ibid., p. 23.
3. G. Edward Griffin, audiotaped interview of, *New Money for Old,* (Hesperia, CA: "Let's Talk About America"), 15 minute cassette No. P12S5.
4. Ibid.

5. Norman Dodd, videotaped interview of, *The Hidden Agenda: Merging America Into World Government,* (Westlake Village, CA: American Media), one hour (VHS)

6. Ibid.

7. Howard E. Kershner, *Dividing The Wealth: Are you Getting your Share?* (Old Greenwich, CT: Devin-Adair Company, 1971), p. 17-19.

8. Lord Curzon, *The Unseen Hand* (Tucson, AZ: Publius Press 1985), p. 261.

9. Perloff, p. 65.

Chapter 11. Babylon's War Against God

1. Michael Kenny, *No God Next Door* (New York, NY: William J. Hirten Co. Inc., 1935), p. 55-56

2. Ibid., p. 65.

3. Ibid., p. 3.

4. William H. McIllhany, *Journal of Individualist Studies* Vol 1, No. 2 (Beverly Hills, CA: Individualist Research Foundation 1992), p. 115.

5. James Thornton, "A Land Where God Is Banned," *The New American,* December 22,

1986. p. 23.

6. Ibid., p. 23.

7. Lev Alburt, audiotaped interview of, *Life in the Soviet Union,(* Hesperia, CA: "Let's Talk About America"), 15 minute cassette No. P3S6.

8. Ibid.

9. David B. Funderburk, audiotaped interview of, *Conditions in Romania and Eastern Europe,* (Hesperia, CA: "Let's Talk About America)," 15 minute cassette No. P8S7.

10. Ibid.

11. James Perloff, "Soldier Statesman, Sage," *The New American,* October 26, 1987. p. 36.

12. Ibid., p. 39.

13. Ibid., p. 38.

14. Ibid., p. 40.

15. Ibid., p. 40

16. Anthony G. Bryant, audiotaped interview of, *Life in Communist Cuba,* (Hesperia, CA: "Let's Talk About America"), 15 minute cassette No. P1S3.

17. Anastasio Somoza, as told to Jack Cox, *Nicaragua Betrayed* (Appleton, WI: Western Islands, 1980), p.206.

18. David Courson, audiotaped interview of, *Marxist Persecution of Christians in Nicaragua,* (Hesperia, CA: "Let's Talk About America"), 15 minute cassette No. P2S3.

19. Peter Hammond, audiotaped interview of, *Communist Terror in Africa,* (Hesperia, CA: "Let's Talk About America"), 15 minute cassette No. P1S7.

20. Ibid.

21. Donald McAlvany, "The African National Congress," *The New American,* August 25, 1986. p. 20.

22. Ibid., p. 20.

23. Ibid., p. 24.

24. Abdul Shams, audiotaped interview of *Soviet Terror in Afghanistan,* (Hesperia, CA: "Let's Talk About America"), 15 minute cassette No. P10S6.

25. William F. Jasper, "How to Create an Islamic Enemy," *The New American,* March 21, 1994. p. 15.

26. William Norman Grigg, "Christianity as a Cult." *The New American,* August 23, 1993. p.33.

Chapter 12. U. N. Modern Tower of Babel

1. James Perloff, *The Shadows of Power; The Council on Foreign Relations And the American Decline* (Appleton, WI: Western Islands, 1990), p. 73.

2. Tomas Schuman, audiotaped interview of, *The Communist Four Step Program to Destroy America,* (Hesperia, CA: "Let's Talk About America"), 15 minute cassette No. P1S1.

3. Ibid.

4. Steven Mosher, audiotaped interview of, *China and Tianamen Square,* (Hesperia, CA: "Let's Talk About America"), 15 minute cassette No. P6S7.

5. William F. Jasper, *Global Tyranny . . . Step By Step: The United Nations and the Emerging New World Order* (Appleton, WI: Western Islands, 1992), p. 265.

6. Dixy Lee Ray, *Environmental Overkill: Whatever Happened To Common Sense?* (Washington, D.C.: Regnery Gateway, 1993), p. 10.

7. Ibid., p. 6.

8. Ibid., p. 7.
9. Ibid., p. 49.
10. Ibid., p. 35.
11. Ibid., p. 34.

Chapter 13. A New Movement in History

1. James Thornton, "Remembering Robert Welch," *The New American,* December 13, 1993. p. 28.
2. John F. McManus, audiotaped interview of, *The Insiders,* (Hesperia, CA: "Let's Talk About America"), 15 minute cassette No. P12S3.
3. Thomas Hill in a speech before the 35th Anniversary JBS Council Dinner, Indianapolis, Indiana, November 13, 1993, (Appleton WI: The John Birch Society)
4. G. Edward Griffin, audiotaped interview of, *Individualism vs Collectivism,* (Hesperia, CA: "Let's Talk About America"), 15 minute cassette No. P8S1.
5. James and Marti Hefley, *The Secret File on John Birch,* (Wheaton, Illinois: Tyndale House Publishers, Inc. 1980), p. 9.

6. Bill Miller in a speech before The Robert Welch Club, Indianapolis, Indiana, November 13, 1993, 9Appleton WI: The John Birch Society)

Chapter 14. The Soul of Babylon

1. James Strong, *Strongs's Exhaustive Concordance,* (Tulsa, Oklahoma, American Christian College Press), p. 75.
2. Joseph D. Douglass, Jr., *Red Cocaine: The Drugging of America,* (Atlanta, Georgia, Clarion House, Inc. 1990), p. xvii.
3. Ibid., pp. xviii - ix.
4. Ibid., p. 8.
5. Ibid., p. 11.
6. Ibid., p. 27.
7. Strong, p. 59.
8. William F. Jasper, "A New World Religion," *The New American,* October 19, 1992. p. 30.
9. William F. Jasper, *Global Tyranny . . . Step By Step: The United Nations and the Emerging New World Order,* (Appleton, WI: Western Islands, 1992), pp. 213-213.

199

10. Clarence Kelly, *Conspiracy Against God And Man,* (Appleton WI: Western Islands 1974), p. 179.

11. Tal Brooke, *When the World Will Be As One* (Eugene, OR: Harvest House Publishers, 1989), pp. 175-176

12. William F. Jasper, "A New World Religion," *The New American,* October 19, 1992. p. 25.

13. Ibid., p. 29.

14. Constance E. Cumbey, *The Hidden Dangers Of The Rainbow:The New Age Movement and Our Coming Age of Barbarism,* (Lafayette, LA: Huntington House, Inc. 1983), pp. 54-55.

15. Ibid., pp. 57-58.

16. Ibid., p. 56.

17. William F. Jasper, *Global Tyranny . . . Step By Step: The United Nations and the Emerging New World Order,* (Appleton Wi: Western Islands, 1992), p. 229.

18. Ibid., p. 229.

19. William F. Jasper, "Death March to Cairo," *The New American,* June 27, 1994. p. 7.

Chapter 15. The Fall of Babylon

1. William F. Jasper, *Global Tyranny . . . Step By Step: The United Nations and the Emerging New world Order,* (Appleton, WI: Western Islands, 1992), p. xvii.

Chapter 16. Conclusions

1. Frederic Bastiat, *The Law* (Irvington-On-Hudson, New York: 1984), p. 6.

2. Ibid., p. 7

3. Ibid., p. 73.

Bibliography

Bastiat, Frederick. *The Law.* Irving-On-Hudson, NY: The Foundation for Economic Education, 1950.

Cumbey, Constance E. *The Hidden Dangers Of The Rainbow: The New Age Movement And Our Coming Age Of Barbarism.* Lafayette, LA: Huntington House, Inc., 1983

Douglass, Joseph D. *Red Cocaine: The Drugging of America.* Atlanta, GA: Clarion House, 1990.

Eidsmoe, John. *Christianity And The Constitution: The Faith of Our Founding Fathers.* Grand Rapids, MI: Baker Book House, 1987.

Flynn, John T. *While You Slept: Our Tragedy In Asia And Who Made It.* Appleton, WI: American Opinion, 1961.

Griffin, G. Edward. *World Without Cancer: The Story of Vitamin B17.* Westlake Village, CA: American Media, 1974.

Griffin, G. Edward. *The Life And Words Of Robert Welch Founder of The John Birch Society.* Westlake Village, CA: American Media, 1975.

Halley, Henry H. *Halley's Bible Handbook.* Grand Rapids, MI: Zondervan Publishing House, 1989.

Hefley, James & Marti. *The Secret File On John Birch.* Wheaton, Il: Tyndale House Publishers, Inc., 1980.

Hoar, William P. *Architects Of Conspiracy: An Intriguing History.* Appleton, WI: Western Islands, 1984.

Jasper, William F. *Global Tyranny . . . Step By Step: The United Nations and the Emerging New World Order.* Appleton WI: Western Islands, 1992.

Kelly, Clarence. *Conspiracy Against God And Man.* Appleton, WI: Western Islands, 1974.

Kenny Michael. *No God Next Door.* New York, NY: William J. Hirten Co. 1935.

Kershner, Howard E. *Dividing The Wealth: Are You Getting Your Share?* Old Greenwich, CT: Devin-Adair Company, 1971.

Marx, Karl. *The Communist Manifesto.* Chicago, IL: Henry Regnery Company, 1969.

McIlhany, William H. *Journal of Individualist Studies Vol. 1, No. 2.* Beverly, Hills, CA: Individualist Research Foundation, 1992.

McManus, John F. *The Insiders.* Appleton, WI: The John Birch Society, 1983.

McManus, John F. *Financial Terrorism: Hijacking America Under the Threat of Bankruptcy.* Appleton, WI: The John Birch Society, 1993.

Perloff, James. *The Shadows of Power: The Council on Foreign Relations and The American Decline.* Appleton, WI: Western Islands, 1988.

Ray, Dixy Lee, *Environmental Overkill: What Ever Happened To Common Sense?* Washington, D. C.: Regnery Gateway, 1993.

Robison, John. *Proofs of a Conspiracy.* Appleton WI: Western Islands, 1967.

Shams, Abdul. *In Cold Blood: The Communist Conquest of Afghanistan.* Appleton,WI: Western Islands, 1987.

Somoza, Anastasio. *Nicaragua Betrayed.* Appleton, WI: Western Islands, 1980.

Sutton, Antony C. *The Best Enemy Money Can Buy.* Billings, MT: Liberty House Press, 1986.

Sutton, Antony C. *Wall Street And The Bolshevik Revolution.* New Rochelle, NY: Arlington House Publishers, 1974.

Weaver, Henry Grady. *The Mainspring of Human Progress.* Irvington-On-Hudson, NY: The Foundation For Economic Education, Inc., 1947.

Webster, Nesta H. *The French Revolution.* Costa Mesa, CA: The Noontide Press, 1992.

Webster, Nesta H. *Secret Societies and Subversive Movements.* Christian Book Club of America.

Welch, Robert. *Again, May God Forgive Us*. Chicago, Il: Henry Regnery Company, 1952.

Welch, Robert. *The Blue Book of The John Birch Society*. Appleton, WI: The John Birch Society, 1959.

Welch, Robert. *The Romance Of Education*. Appleton, WI: Western Islands, 1973.

Articles and Reports

Alburt, Lev. (audiotaped interview of). *Life in the Soviet Union*. Hesperia, CA: "Let's Talk About America," 15 minute cassette.

Bryant, Anthony. (audiotaped interview of). *Life in Communist Cuba*. Hesperia, CA: "Let's Talk About America," 15 minute cassette.

Carlson, Charles. "Attacking Islam," *The New American*, March 21, 1994.

Courson, David. (audiotaped interview of). *Marxist Persecution of Christians in Nicaragua*. Hesperia, CA: "Let'sTalk About America," 15 minute cassette.

Funderburk, David B. (audiotaped interview of). *Conditions in Romania and Eastern Europe*. Hesperia, CA: "Let's Talk About America," 15 minute cassette.

Griffin, G. Edward. (audiotaped interview of). *Individualism vs Collectivism*. Hesperia, CA: "Let's Talk About America," 15 minute cassette.

Griffin, G. Edward. (audiotaped interview of). *New Money for Old*. Hesperia, CA: "Let's Talk About America," 15 minute cassette.

Grigg, William Norman. "Christianity as a 'Cult,'" *The New American*, August 23, 1993.

Hammond, Peter. (audiotaped interview of). *Communist Terror in Africa.* Hesperia, CA: "Let's Talk About America," 15 minute cassette.

Hill, Thomas. "Reflections about the John Birch Society." An address delivered at the 35th aniversity JBS Council Dinner. Nov. 13, 1993. The John Birch society, Appleton, WI.

Jasper, William F. "A New World Religion," *The New American, October 19, 1992.*

Jasper, William F. "Death March to Cairo," *The New American,* June 27, 1994.

McAlvany, Donald S. "The African National Congress," *The New American,* August 25, 1986.

McIlhany, William H. "Evidence of a Master Conspiracy," transcript of a filmed lecture. Beverly Hills, CA: Individualist Research Foundation, 1987.

McManus, John F. (audiotaped interview of). *The Insiders.* Hesperia, CA: "Let's Talk About America," 15 min cassette.

Miller, William. "The Communist Mudrer of John Birch." An address delivered at the Robert Welch Club. Nov. 13, 1993. The John Birch Society, Appleton, WI.

Mosher, Steven. (audiotaped interview of). *China and Tiananmen Square.* Hesperia, CA: "Let's Talk About America," 15 minute cassette.

Perloff, James "Soldier, Statesman, Sage," *The New American,* October 26, 1987.

Schuman, Tomas (audiotaped interview of). *The Commusist Four-Step Program to Destroy America.* Hesperia, CA: "Let's Talk About America," 15 minute cassette.

Shams, Abdul (audiotaped interview of). *Soviet Terror in Afghanistan.* Hesperia, CA: "Let's Talk About America," 15 minute cassette.

Thornton, James "A Land Where God Is Banned," *The New American,* December 22, 1986.

Thornton, James "Remembering Robert Welch," *The NewAmerican,* December 13, 1993.

Index

The Secret Side of History
on audio cassettes

▸ Three C90 cassettes with attractive album holder enables you to hear the actual voices of 14 people quoted in the *Secret Side of History* including such authorities as Norman Dodd, G. Edward Griffin, John McManus, Steven Mosher, Lev Alburt, and many others.

▸ Audio Book price includes shipping $15.00

Also available

▸ Twelve 15 minute "Let's Talk About America" radio programs on cassette tape. Enables you to hear the full 15 minute programs quoted from in *The Secret Side of History.*

▸ Let's Talk About America 15 minute cassette $5.00
The Secret Side of History single copy $10.00
The Secret Side of History 5 or more . . . . . .$6.00 ea.
Please add $2.00 for shipping. in Calif add 7¾% tax

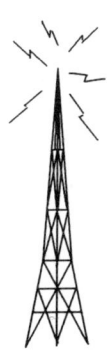

order from

LTAA Communications
P. O. Box 403092
Hesperia, California 92345

ABOUT THE AUTHOR

Dee Zahner is a graduate of what is now Bartlesville Wesleyan College where he majored in theology. He is also a graduate of the Los Angeles County Sheriff's Academy for Reserve Officers and served as a reserve deputy sheriff for ten years. For several years he served as a lay minister at the Little Chapel of the Canyon in the San Gabriel Mountains in Southern California.

In 1982 he became the producer and host of "Let's Talk About America" a weekly series of radio interviews that were eventually heard in 37 states on radio or cassette tapes. "Let's Talk About America" has been aired on seven radio stations in California.

In addition to *The Secret Side of Money: A History of Manipulation,* he is also the author of *The Secret Side of History: Mystery Babylon and the New World Order* and *Gringo and the Coconut* a true human interest story in English and Spanish with a screenplay included.

A small businessman for the past 27 years, he is the owner of LTAA Communications a book publishing and audio production company in Southern California.